Praise For

# *The Gilded Revival*

"An essential guide for professionals in luxury real estate. Mark Satterfield masterfully explains how the renewed prominence of wealth and glamour is transforming the way people dream, purchase, and live."

*— Olivia Kim, Marketing Director, Luxury Real Estate*

"Mark's insights into the cultural resurgence of wealth and ambition make this a must-read for anyone advising clients in the financial sector. It's a roadmap to better understanding their goals and aspirations."

*— Laura Rodriguez, Private Wealth Advisor*

"*The Gilded Revival* is a groundbreaking resource for luxury real estate professionals. It captures how wealth and glamour are shaping the desires we sell—homes that are more than shelters; they're symbols of success and legacy."

*— Sophia Bennett, Luxury Property Specialist*

"In an era of shifting attitudes toward wealth, *The Gilded Revival* offers wealth managers the insights they need to guide their clients with confidence and clarity."

*— Thomas Blake, Managing Director, Financial Services*

"As a wealth manager, understanding client psychology is vital. *The Gilded Revival* provides critical perspectives on today's affluent, helping us forge meaningful connections."

*— David Chu, Senior Partner, Wealth Management*

"This book blends cultural insights with practical strategies, making it a must-have for anyone looking to excel in industries driven by aspiration and exclusivity."

*— Sophia Chang, Concierge Health & Wellness*

"An exceptional exploration of the comeback of wealth and glamour in modern culture. *The Gilded Revival* is an insightful guide for serving clients who value style, success, and sophistication."

*— William Carter, Luxury Travel & Hospitality*

"*The Gilded Revival* reshapes how wealth managers think about success. It's not just about managing resources but connecting with the ambitions that drive affluent individuals forward."

*— Sarah Kim, Wealth Management*

"Mark Satterfield's latest work illuminates the cultural trends redefining the affluent market. It's an indispensable guide for luxury real estate professionals aiming to provide unparalleled service."

*— John Reynolds, Luxury Real Estate*

"This book offers a rare blend of cultural commentary and practical advice, making it invaluable for those who cater to the affluent. A true masterpiece."

*— Marcus Lee, Fine Art & Collectibles*

"A captivating journey through the resurgence of wealth and glamour in American culture. *The Gilded Revival* is both an insightful analysis and a practical guide for excelling in this evolving landscape."

*— Emma Carter, Luxury Travel Consultant*

# The Gilded Revival

## America's Return to
### an Age of Wealth & Glamour

**MARK SATTERFIELD**

Copyright © 2024 Mark Satterfield

ISBN: 979-8-9876017-9-2

Published by Mandalay Press



Book cover design & typesetting by manuscript2ebook.com

To my wife Marian,
for all her love, support
and encouragement.

Discover how your business can effectively attract
and engage affluent clients.

# Table of Contents

Reflecting on the values, symbols, and impact of America's return to wealth and glamour. How will history view the Gilded Revival?

# Introduction

There's a moment in American history when the country felt like it was on the edge of something extraordinary—a time when wealth was not just a dream but a visible, tangible reality. This period, known as the Gilded Age, saw the rise of some of the richest men and women the world had ever known. But it wasn't just about the dollars and cents; it was about what wealth represented: power, influence, and the possibility of reinvention.

Fast forward to today, and something remarkably similar is happening again. We find ourselves in the midst of a new Gilded Age, where the pursuit of wealth is no longer hidden or hushed. Instead, it's celebrated—displayed on social media, broadcast across TV screens, and woven into the very fabric of our culture. But what exactly has sparked this return to a time when financial success and glamour seemed to be everything?

In this book, we're diving into the reasons behind America's reemergence as a land where wealth is not only created at unprecedented rates but is also flaunted in ways that are impossible to ignore. We'll explore the powerhouses of today—the tech moguls, the media icons, and the CEOs who have redefined what it means to be successful in a world where image, influence, and money intersect like never before.

## A Look Back at the Past

To understand how we got here, we need to look back at the last time America was engulfed in an era of financial glamour—the late 19th century. It was a time of breathtaking wealth, driven by industrial giants like John D. Rockefeller, Andrew Carnegie, and J.P. Morgan. These men weren't just businessmen; they were the architects of a new world. Imagine living in an era when Rockefeller controlled nearly all of the oil in the country and Carnegie owned more steel than anyone else in the world. The sheer scale of their fortunes was mind-boggling.

But their success came at a cost. While these men built empires, workers labored long hours in dangerous conditions, and cities became overcrowded, unsanitary, and rife with poverty. It was a time of extremes—the Gilded Age—where the glittering gold of wealth masked the inequality that was festering beneath the surface.

Today, we are witnessing a similar rise in wealth, but this time it's happening in the digital age. Thanks to tech giants like Elon Musk, Jeff Bezos, and Mark Zuckerberg, the world's richest individuals are creating fortunes on a scale that rivals the industrial titans of the past. In fact, the fortunes made by these modern moguls are often much more visible, thanks to the rise of social media and the 24-hour news cycle.

## The World of Tech and Titans

Look no further than the meteoric rise of Silicon Valley for proof of this new Gilded Age. Consider Elon Musk, who turned a series of wild, visionary ideas into a multi-billion-dollar empire, starting with PayPal and going on to create Tesla, SpaceX, and Neuralink. Musk has become a celebrity in his own right, blending the roles of tech genius, media figure, and modern-day inventor. His personal brand is as much a part of his success as his companies, and his influence over the culture of innovation and wealth is undeniable.

Then there's Jeff Bezos, the man who redefined shopping and completely transformed the way we consume goods. Amazon started as an online bookstore in 1994, and now it's a global juggernaut, touching nearly every aspect of modern life. Bezos's rise to wealth and power has had ripple effects across industries and cultures, just as Mark Zuckerberg has changed the way we connect and communicate, building a company that owns Facebook, Instagram, and WhatsApp, and influencing billions of people worldwide.

These modern titans share a common trait with the industrial moguls of the past: they don't just create wealth—they shape culture. Their ideas, their companies, and their personal brands have turned them into icons of the 21st century.

## The Glitter and the Grit

But it's not all about the billionaires. It's also about the shift in how we view wealth. Today, thanks to the rise of social media, even ordinary people can showcase their success and the lifestyle that comes with it. Think about Instagram—a platform where luxury cars, exotic vacations, and high-end fashion are paraded for the world to see. A picture of a private jet or a luxury mansion is no longer something reserved for the ultra-rich. Now, anyone can curate an image of wealth and glamour—and millions of people follow it.

Take, for instance, Kim Kardashian, a woman who built an empire based on personal branding. Through her reality show, social media presence, and businesses like KKW Beauty, she's shown us how to monetize not just a product, but a lifestyle. And in doing so, she's become a symbol of how wealth can be democratized in the digital age. It's no longer just about who you are but about how you present yourself.

Yet, just like the Gilded Age, there's still an undercurrent of inequality. As the rich continue to rise, many are left behind. Workers in gig economies, factory jobs, and service industries are still struggling, while the top 1% continues to accumulate wealth. It's a reminder that while the glitter of wealth may shine brighter than ever, the struggles beneath the surface remain much the same.

## The Future of the Gilded Revival

So, what does all of this mean for the future? Can this new Gilded Age sustain itself, or will it eventually crack under the pressure of inequality, climate change, and political unrest? One thing's for certain: we're witnessing the birth of a new kind of wealth and power, one that blends technology, entertainment, and personal branding into something more dynamic and visible than ever before.

This book will take you on a journey through this new era of financial glamour. From the rise of Silicon Valley to the power of social media, from the tech moguls to the media influencers, we'll explore the people and trends that are shaping our world. Along the way, we'll examine the legacies of those who came before us—the industrialists and moguls who set the stage for what we're experiencing today.

It's an era where wealth is no longer just about money; it's about influence, visibility, and the stories we tell. This is America's return to a world where financial success is the ultimate status symbol, and the drive to achieve it is as strong as ever.

Welcome to the Gilded Revival—where wealth and glamour are no longer just for the few but for anyone bold enough to chase them.

# Echoes of the Past: America's Original Gilded Age

Imagine stepping into a world where wealth is not just a means of comfort but the ultimate aspiration—a time when the rich didn't just live differently, they lived grandly. The late 19th century in America, known as the Gilded Age, was just that. It was an era defined by extraordinary wealth, opulent lifestyles, and an insatiable drive to build and acquire. From towering mansions on Fifth Avenue to extravagant dinner parties filled with the country's most influential people, this was a time when the pursuit of wealth shaped the very identity of the nation.

But what does this era have to do with today? The truth is, America's original Gilded Age set the stage for much of what we see in the modern world—a world that increasingly celebrates success, wealth, and luxury in ways that are bigger, bolder, and more visible than ever. The glimmering gold of the Gilded Age may have faded, but its cultural legacy is alive and well in the 21st century.

In this chapter, we'll journey back to this fascinating period, looking at the rise of the industrial titans who built their fortunes on oil, steel, and railroads, as well as the social elite who became symbols of America's new era of wealth. We'll explore how figures like John D. Rockefeller, Andrew Carnegie, and Cornelius Vanderbilt didn't just accumulate wealth—they shaped an entire culture of excess and ambition.

But while the industrialists were creating their empires, there was something deeper at play. The Gilded Age wasn't just about making money; it was about making a statement. It was about living in a way that reflected power, influence, and success on a scale never before seen in American history. This period gave birth to a fascination with luxury and high status—values that still dominate our culture today.

So why does the Gilded Age matter now? Simply put, the echoes of that time can still be heard in today's society. Whether it's the rise of tech moguls like Elon Musk or Mark Zuckerberg, or the explosion of influencer culture on social media, we're seeing a re-emergence of the same values that defined the original Gilded Age: the quest for wealth, the desire for visibility, and the belief that success is something to be flaunted.

As we look back at the foundations of the first Gilded Age, we'll uncover not just the fortunes made, but the cultural shifts that forever changed how we view money, success, and what it means to be truly rich. The past and present are more connected than they may seem—and in understanding the original Gilded Age, we gain a clearer picture of today's Gilded Revival.

## Chapter 1.1: The Dawn of Wealth in America: Industrialization and Innovation

In the second half of the 19th century, America was on the brink of something truly extraordinary. The pace of change was dizzying, and nowhere was this more apparent than in the world of business and industry. It was a time when railroads stretched across the vastness of the country, steel bridges began to span great rivers, and factories churned out goods faster than anyone could have imagined. The Industrial Revolution had taken hold, and the transformation it wrought would change the course of American history forever.

The Industrial Revolution of the late 19th century was more than just a technological shift. It was a societal transformation—a movement that radically redefined the way people lived, worked, and even dreamed. The rural, agrarian society that had once defined America was rapidly giving way to a new urbanized, industrialized world, fueled by the rise of massive factories, new transportation systems, and the mass production of goods. It was an era where innovation was king, and the opportunities for wealth and progress seemed endless.

## A New Age of Innovation

America had already witnessed a few bursts of technological innovation earlier in its history, but nothing compared to the seismic shifts that would take place during the late 1800s. The Industrial Revolution didn't just bring new machines—it introduced entirely new ways of thinking about work, production, and business.

One of the most profound changes was the rise of the factory system. Powered by the advent of steam engines and innovations in machinery, factories could now produce goods at a speed and scale that was unprecedented. This was the dawn of mass production. Instead of individual craftsmen painstakingly making goods by hand, factories could now churn out products in large quantities. The assembly line, still a concept in its early stages, would eventually revolutionize manufacturing, especially in industries like automobiles and textiles.

At the heart of this transformation was transportation. The expansion of the railroad system was nothing short of revolutionary. Railroads became the arteries of the American economy, allowing goods and people to move faster and farther than ever before. The completion of the Transcontinental Railroad in 1869, which connected the East and West coasts of the United States, symbolized the triumph of industrial ambition. Suddenly, it was possible to ship raw materials across the country to factories and deliver finished goods to new markets far and wide.

Railroads created vast new opportunities for commerce and trade, shaping the very foundation of American capitalism.

In tandem with these advancements came the development of a new infrastructure to support this industrial growth. Cities grew rapidly as people moved from rural farms to urban centers in search of factory work. Skyscrapers began to rise, signaling the dawn of urbanization and the coming shift in American life. The streets that had once been filled with horse-drawn carriages became crowded with streetcars and trains, bustling with people who were part of a new economic order that was moving at a breakneck speed.

## The Rise of the Titans

But while the factories, railroads, and infrastructure were expanding at an unprecedented rate, it wasn't just technology that was reshaping America. There were also the men—the visionaries and the entrepreneurs—who would come to define the era. These were the first financial titans of America, the men who took full advantage of the new industrial landscape and amassed fortunes that would lay the groundwork for the modern economy.

Andrew Carnegie is one of the most iconic figures of the Gilded Age. Born to poor Scottish immigrants in 1835, Carnegie's rise to power was nothing short of miraculous. Starting as a bobbin boy in a cotton factory, he worked his way up through the ranks, eventually founding the Carnegie Steel Company in the 1870s. With the rapid expansion of railroads and infrastructure, Carnegie's steel was in high demand. He became the largest producer of steel in the world, and by the time he sold his company to J.P. Morgan in 1901, Carnegie's personal wealth had ballooned to more than $300 million—equivalent to billions in today's money. Carnegie's success was built on his ability to innovate within the steel industry, using vertical integration to control every aspect of production, from raw materials to finished products.

Then there was John D. Rockefeller, who built an empire in the oil industry. Rockefeller's journey to the top started with a small oil refinery in Cleveland in 1863. Through ruthless business tactics and strategic acquisitions, Rockefeller founded Standard Oil, which would eventually control over 90% of the oil refining capacity in the United States. Rockefeller's influence was so immense that he became the wealthiest man in the world. His fortune—over $400 billion in today's dollars—made him a symbol of wealth, power, and sometimes controversy. His monopoly on oil sparked fierce competition and led to the first major antitrust action in American history, as the government sought to break up his monopoly to ensure fair competition. Yet, despite this, Rockefeller's legacy as one of the wealthiest men ever to live remains.

While Carnegie and Rockefeller made their fortunes in industry, J.P. Morgan was the man who helped finance their empires. Born into a wealthy banking family, Morgan became one of the most powerful financiers of his time. He was instrumental in consolidating and reorganizing American industries, merging corporations to create larger, more efficient entities. In 1901, Morgan's U.S. Steel became the first billion-dollar corporation in the world, and Morgan's influence over the financial markets made him a key player in shaping the modern economy.

Additionally, there was Cornelius Vanderbilt, who made his fortune in railroads and shipping. Starting as a steamship operator, Vanderbilt eventually shifted his focus to railroads, building one of the largest railroad empires in America. His aggressive expansion and consolidation of railroads earned him the nickname "The Commodore," and by the time of his death in 1877, his fortune was one of the largest in the country. Vanderbilt's railroads transformed the American landscape, making it possible for goods to travel across vast distances more quickly and efficiently than ever before.

These men were the first of a new class of American titans, their fortunes built on innovation, bold risk-taking, and often, sheer willpower.

They were the individuals who personified the new era, setting the standard for what it meant to be successful in the Gilded Age. Their wealth gave them not just power over industries but influence over politics, society, and culture.

## The New American Dream: A Single Generation of Wealth

What made the Gilded Age truly unique wasn't just the scale of the fortunes—it was the speed with which they were amassed. For the first time in American history, it was possible for a single individual to go from humble beginnings to extraordinary wealth within their lifetime. This was the birth of a new version of the American Dream—one that was no longer about land or opportunity, but about the ability to create wealth out of nothing.

Before the Gilded Age, many Americans were born into inherited wealth, or they spent their entire lives working the land in rural settings. But the industrial revolution changed that. People from all walks of life now had the opportunity to rise to the top through sheer ambition and entrepreneurial spirit. The dream of accumulating wealth quickly and achieving success in a single lifetime became the driving force behind the nation's economic expansion.

The myth of the self-made man—the idea that anyone could rise from humble beginnings to great wealth—was more than just a romantic notion in the Gilded Age. It was a reality for many of the era's most famous industrialists. Carnegie, Rockefeller, Morgan, and Vanderbilt were all products of this new American ethos: that with hard work, innovation, and a bit of luck, anything was possible.

This new version of the American Dream did more than change the way people thought about success—it changed what people aspired to. The Gilded Age introduced a culture of luxury, opulence, and affluence that would shape American society for decades to come. The wealth accumulated by the industrialists wasn't just about power—it was about living in ways that displayed their success. Mansions, private railcars, luxury yachts—these became the symbols of wealth, the markers that set the rich apart from the rest of society.

As the industrial giants built their fortunes, they also built a culture that glorified wealth. This wasn't just about economic success—it was about living the kind of life that everyone else dreamed of, flaunting it for the world to see. And as the wealth gap grew, so did the cultural fascination with wealth. This created a framework for future generations to follow—a framework that persists to this day, as we see the rise of a new generation of billionaires who flaunt their success in ways that echo the excesses of the Gilded Age.

In the end, the Gilded Age was more than just a period of industrial growth; it was a cultural revolution. It redefined what it meant to be successful in America, laying the foundation for the country's ongoing fascination with wealth, luxury, and the pursuit of financial power. And in many ways, the echoes of that era are still shaping our world today. The lessons learned, the values instilled, and the icons created in the Gilded Age continue to resonate—whispering their influence into our modern pursuit of wealth and success.

## Chapter 1.2: Defining the Gilded Age: Wealth, Glamour, and Socioeconomic Contrast

The late 19th century in America was a time of paradox. On the one hand, it was an era of remarkable economic expansion, technological innovation, and an unprecedented accumulation of wealth. On the other hand, it was an era marked by stark socioeconomic contrasts, where the ultra-wealthy reveled in opulence, while the vast majority of Americans struggled with poverty, child labor, and harsh working conditions. This contrast between extreme wealth and widespread poverty became one of the defining features of what we now call the Gilded Age—an age where the pursuit of wealth and the display of luxury became central to the American identity.

The term "Gilded Age," coined by Mark Twain, originally carried a hint of irony, suggesting that while the surface glittered with gold, much of what lay beneath was tarnished and hollow. Yet, in many ways, the age was as glittering as Twain described. For the ultra-wealthy, this period was a time of excess and indulgence in every aspect of life—from the homes they lived in, to the clothes they wore, to the parties they threw. At the same time, the luxury class was not just about enjoying wealth in private—it was about flaunting success, creating a visible, almost theatrical spectacle of wealth. This chapter delves into how the Gilded Age became synonymous with glamour and how the wealthy built the foundations for much of the cultural infrastructure we see today.

## Opulence and Excess: The Lifestyle of the Ultra-Wealthy

To understand the opulence of the Gilded Age, you have to picture a world where money was no longer just about security—it was about status. And that status had to be shown, displayed, and celebrated at every turn. This was the era of lavish mansions, elaborate balls, and fancy fashions, where the wealthiest Americans lived lives of unparalleled grandeur.

**Mansions and Estates**: For the new rich of the Gilded Age, the size and extravagance of one's home were the ultimate indicators of success. Cities like New York, Newport, and Philadelphia became dotted with mansions that were the epitome of extravagance. The Vanderbilt mansion on Fifth Avenue in New York, for example, was a 13-story marvel of wealth, featuring a private art gallery, a grand ballroom, and golden chandeliers. Built at a cost of $12 million (over $300 million in today's dollars), it was the epitome of what wealth could buy—a private palace for the elite to both live in and show off. The Vanderbilts were not alone in building such monumental homes; other wealthy families followed suit, creating homes that were not only a display of personal fortune but a way to say, "We have arrived, and we will not be overlooked."

Meanwhile, the mansions in Newport, Rhode Island, became known as the "summer cottages" of the American elite, where families like the Astors and Morgans built their grand estates along the coast. These sprawling, palatial homes—many designed in the Beaux-Arts or Gothic Revival styles—were constructed with the finest materials, often imported from Europe. These homes were not just places of residence, but monuments to the industrialists' success. They were places to entertain, places to display wealth, and places that screamed opulence at the highest level.

**Fashion and Appearance**: If the mansions were the backdrop, the clothing was the canvas on which the elite painted their social status. Fashion in the Gilded Age was all about extravagance and attention to detail. The wealthy donned tailored suits, silk dresses, and diamond jewelry, their clothing becoming an extension of their wealth. Women of high society wore gowns made from the finest fabrics, often hand-embroidered with gold thread or encrusted with diamonds. For men, the traditional morning coat was the standard at high-society events, a garment that was as much about displaying wealth as it was about conforming to social norms. No detail was too small to escape scrutiny, and the display of wealth through fashion became an integral part of the social theater of the time.

**Social Gatherings**: The display of wealth didn't stop at the home or the wardrobe—it extended to the events and gatherings that defined high society life. Ballrooms in New York and Newport hosted lavish parties that could cost millions of dollars in today's money, with elaborate decorations, extravagant catering, and live orchestras. These gatherings were more than just parties—they were opportunities to demonstrate power, to network with the elite, and to make sure that everyone knew who you were. The Astor and Vanderbilt families were especially known for hosting some of the most spectacular balls of the period. These events were carefully orchestrated, with the wealthiest families in attendance, all trying to outdo each other in terms of extravagance. One such affair, hosted by Caroline Astor, invited only the elite of New York society and was widely considered the pinnacle of refinement.

The goal of these parties was not only to entertain but to confirm the social hierarchy of the time. For many of the wealthy, these events were about maintaining control over the status quo, ensuring that their place at the top of the social ladder was secure.

## The Rise of Cultural Institutions: Investing in Legacy

As the wealth of the industrial magnates grew, so too did their desire to shape culture and leave a legacy that went beyond just money. The Gilded Age was a time when the ultra-wealthy began to invest in cultural institutions—museums, universities, libraries, and art galleries—that would serve as lasting symbols of their wealth, intellect, and benevolence.

**Philanthropy:** The Gilded Age saw the birth of philanthropy on an unprecedented scale. Figures like Andrew Carnegie and John D. Rockefeller, who amassed fortunes through their business ventures, began to direct a significant portion of their wealth to charitable causes. Carnegie, for instance, gave away over $350 million to causes ranging from libraries to universities. One of his most well-known contributions was the funding of public libraries across America. His belief that "a man who dies rich dies disgraced" became the driving philosophy behind his philanthropic efforts. Carnegie's legacy of giving included the establishment of Carnegie Mellon University in Pittsburgh, a cultural landmark that continues to be a symbol of academic and intellectual prestige.

**Museums and Cultural Landmarks:** The ultra-wealthy also took a keen interest in investing in and creating cultural landmarks that would stand as testaments to their status. The Metropolitan Museum of Art in

New York City, for example, was significantly funded by wealthy patrons, with families like the Rockefellers and the Morgans making substantial contributions. The museum, which opened in 1872, was not just a collection of art—it was a reflection of the elite's desire to cultivate culture in the same way they cultivated wealth. Their investments in art and architecture helped lay the foundation for institutions that have become synonymous with America's rich cultural heritage.

Another significant example is the creation of the Carnegie Hall in 1891. Initially funded by Andrew Carnegie, this iconic music venue became a focal point for the performing arts in New York City and remains one of the most prestigious concert halls in the world. Like many of the Gilded Age's investments, Carnegie Hall was as much about creating a cultural landmark as it was about reinforcing the social standing of its benefactor.

Similarly, the Gilded Age saw the establishment of other enduring institutions like Yale University, Princeton University, and the Rockefeller Institute for Medical Research. These institutions not only provided education and advancement in various fields but also further solidified the wealthy's role as the guardians of culture and knowledge in America.

## The Birth of the New American Dream

Perhaps one of the most important outcomes of the Gilded Age was the transformation of the American Dream. In the years following the Civil War, it became possible, for the first time, for individuals to accumulate vast wealth within their own lifetimes. The rise of the industrial magnates and their ability to create multi-million-dollar empires turned the notion of the self-made man into more than a myth—it became a reality.

This new American Dream was no longer just about owning land or achieving success through hard work—it was about acquiring wealth on a scale that allowed individuals to live lives of luxury and opulence. The pursuit of wealth became entangled with the pursuit of status, and wealth itself became synonymous with glamour. It was about more than just financial success—it was about being seen and recognized by society as the best, the most powerful, and the most successful.

As we move further into the 20th century and beyond, we can trace much of the cultural fascination with wealth, glamour, and luxury to this moment in history. The Gilded Age was the birth of the world we live in today, a world where status, wealth, and power are often displayed as public spectacles, with media and social platforms amplifying the messages of those who have succeeded. And while the wealth of the Gilded Age may have been concentrated in the hands of a few, its impact on American culture was universal. Today's billionaires and moguls are, in many ways, the heirs of the Gilded Age's legacy—living out a version of the American Dream built on the foundations of wealth, glamour, and the desire to leave a legacy that will endure for generations.

## Chapter 1.3: The Power of Public Perception and the Birth of the Wealth Icon

In the late 19th century, a new cultural phenomenon emerged, one that was fueled by the enormous wealth generated by industrialists, financiers, and entrepreneurs. This was the age when the wealthy elite were no longer content with just accumulating riches in the shadows of industry—they wanted to be seen, celebrated, and admired. Their wealth was no longer just a private possession; it became a public spectacle, intricately woven into the fabric of American society and culture. The newly minted millionaires of the Gilded Age were not only businessmen and women—they were icons of success, symbols of America's boundless possibilities, and aspirational figures for the masses.

During this time, the wealth of the Gilded Age was transformed into cultural capital by media, fashion, and the widespread fascination with the self-made man. The celebrity millionaires who emerged during this period did not just enjoy wealth—they became public figures, their lives becoming stories that were told and retold in newspapers, magazines, and society columns. The Vanderbilts, Astors, and Carnegies were transformed from mere industrialists into legends of wealth, their images ingrained in the public consciousness as models of the American Dream. It was not only their financial accomplishments that captured the imagination of the public—it was how they lived their lives, how they spent their money, and how they appeared to the world.

## Glamour in the Media: The First Celebrity Millionaires

The role of the media in shaping the public's perception of wealth during the Gilded Age cannot be overstated. Newspapers and magazines became the primary vehicles for disseminating the stories of the wealthy, elevating figures like Alva Vanderbilt, Caroline Astor, and Jay Gould to celebrity status. In an era when mass media was still in its infancy, these publications held enormous influence in shaping public opinion and building public personas.

One of the key ways in which media elevated these figures was through society columns, which chronicled the lives and activities of the upper echelons of American society. The New York Times, The New York Herald, and The Social Register all featured regular columns detailing the comings and goings of wealthy families, from the debutante balls to the extravagant galas thrown at lavish estates. These columns allowed the public to peer into the private lives of the rich, creating an almost voyeuristic fascination with their luxurious lifestyles.

For example, Alva Vanderbilt was not only the wife of one of the richest men in America, William Henry Vanderbilt, but also a fashion icon and socialite in her own right. Alva was celebrated for her extravagant parties and lavish fashion choices—her wardrobe filled with European couture. Her parties were chronicled in the press as events that could rival any royal affair. Journalists would describe her ornate ballrooms, the glittering jewels she wore, and the famous guests she entertained, all contributing to her image as a woman whose wealth and status were beyond compare. Alva Vanderbilt became an international symbol of luxury, her name synonymous with high society.

Similarly, Caroline Astor, the matriarch of the prominent Astor family, became one of the most written-about women in America during this time. Her influence was so significant that her social standing became the subject of much public speculation. She was not just an influential figure in New York society; she was considered the gatekeeper of elite circles. To be invited into the Astor's world was to be considered part of the American aristocracy. The press played a major role in perpetuating her image as a symbol of grace, beauty, and wealth. Her role as an arbiter of social taste made her a constant fixture in the media, reinforcing the notion that social success was a mark of financial success.

But it wasn't just women who captured the public's eye. Men like Jay Gould, the railroad magnate, and Cornelius Vanderbilt, the shipping and rail baron, were the subject of intense media coverage. These men were not only business titans but larger-than-life figures, their personal lives dissected as closely as their business dealings. Gould, for example, was frequently depicted as a robber baron, a term that became synonymous with unscrupulous wealth. His image, though tainted by scandal, still captured the public's imagination as he lived a life of wealth and power that many could only dream of. Similarly, Vanderbilt, whose fortune had been built on shipping and railroads, was regularly featured in newspapers as a symbol of the American capitalist who had risen to the top through sheer force of will. The media's portrayal of these figures helped solidify their status as icons of wealth.

## Fashioning the Wealthy Identity: Luxury, Jewelry, and Architectural Extravagance

In the Gilded Age, fashion and luxury became intertwined in a way that had never been seen before. The wealthy were not just content with wearing fine clothing; they sought to make statements of power and status through their appearance. Jewelry, haute couture fashion, and architectural extravagance were tools used to convey their wealth and solidify their position at the top of society.

Fashion was one of the most visible and tangible expressions of wealth during the Gilded Age. Couture houses like Worth in Paris, and American designers like Charles Frederick Worth and Jean-Philippe Worth, designed custom garments for the rich, which were often so exquisite and elaborate that they could only be worn once before being outshined by newer creations. The elite class would regularly display their wealth through elaborate ball gowns, embroidered dresses, and exquisite accessories, all of which were designed to captivate onlookers. It wasn't just about looking good—it was about being seen as part of an exclusive club, one that could afford the finest of everything.

Jewelry, too, played an important role in defining the wealthy identity of the Gilded Age. Diamonds, pearls, and sapphires were the standard, and jewelers, most notably Tiffany & Co. rose to prominence during this time, catering specifically to the demand for luxury. The press often chronicled the jewelry collections of the rich, making Tiffany's synonymous with wealth and sophistication. These jewels weren't just beautiful—they were symbols of status and the sheer power of money.

But it wasn't just clothing and accessories that made the wealthy stand out—it was the homes they built. Architecture became another medium through which the wealthy could express their opulence. Mansions were designed by prominent architects like Richard Morris Hunt and Henry Hobson Richardson, who created grandiose homes with ornate facades, golden trim, and massive proportions. These homes were not just places of residence; they were symbols of wealth and power. The press covered every detail of these estates, from their lavish interiors to their impressive gardens. These homes were the ultimate status symbols, designed to ensure that their owners were seen as untouchable, the epitome of success and luxury.

## Legends of American Success: The Self-Made Man

Perhaps the most enduring symbol of the Gilded Age's wealth culture was the self-made man—the figure who rose from humble beginnings to achieve immense wealth through hard work, ingenuity, and determination. This was the quintessential American Dream, and it was popularized during the Gilded Age in a way that would resonate for generations to come.

Andrew Carnegie, who began life as the son of a poor weaver in Scotland, became one of the richest men in the world through his investments in the steel industry. His story became the archetype of the self-made man, someone who rose from nothing and amassed a fortune through his own hard work and entrepreneurial spirit. Carnegie's rags-to-riches story resonated with millions of Americans who saw him not just as a businessman, but as a model of American ingenuity.

Similarly, John D. Rockefeller, whose rise to power in the oil industry made him the wealthiest man in the world, became an emblem of American success. Rockefeller's story—his early struggles, his innovative approach to business, and his eventual dominance of the oil market—made him an idol of hard work and vision. He, like Carnegie, was held up as an example of how anyone in America could achieve success, regardless of their starting point.

These figures helped solidify the idea that wealth wasn't something that was simply inherited—it was something that could be earned. The media, in turn, played a massive role in crafting these figures into icons of success. Their stories were told again and again, celebrated as the embodiment of American values.

In the end, the Gilded Age was not just an era of industrialization and wealth—it was an era that defined how Americans viewed success, luxury, and the path to greatness. The wealthy elite were no longer just business leaders—they were celebrities, icons, and symbols of the new America, a country where wealth and opulence were as much about perception as they were about reality. Their influence continues to shape the way we view wealth today, and their legacy as the first celebrity millionaires lives on.

## Chapter 1.4: The Cultural Legacy of the Gilded Age

The Gilded Age—a time of grand opulence, extreme wealth, and rapid societal change—has left a lasting cultural legacy that continues to shape the way Americans view success, wealth, and ambition. While the era itself was short-lived, the imprint it left on American society is profound and far-reaching. Today, nearly a century and a half later, echoes of this period reverberate through the fabric of American identity. The glamour, aspiration, and financial success of the Gilded Age are not relics of the past but continue to influence the way Americans define the ideal of the American Dream and how they navigate the complexities of modern-day success.

As we look at the legacy of the Gilded Age, we see the origins of many of the values and cultural elements that are still present in America today. We see the roots of an obsession with wealth, the celebration of self-made success, and the desire for visible opulence that remains firmly embedded in the nation's psyche. The ways in which the wealthy class of the 19th century wielded their wealth, displayed their opulence, and reshaped society through their patronage are lessons that continue to influence today's elite.

In this chapter, we'll explore how the cultural legacy of the original Gilded Age lives on in American society, how it has become interwoven into the modern-day fabric of wealth and success, and whether the Gilded Age has truly been reborn in the 21st century. As we delve into these themes, we'll begin to see how the forces of the past have shaped our present and how the current era, marked by billionaires, tech moguls, and media-driven success stories, may be nothing less than a new iteration of the Gilded Age itself.

## A Lasting Influence on American Values

The Gilded Age was a period that gave birth to the American myth of unrestricted upward mobility, an idea that has come to define the country's social fabric. For the first time, it seemed that wealth and success were not solely the privileges of the established aristocracy. Instead, they were available to anyone with the right combination of vision, work ethic, and, at times, ruthlessness. It was during this time that the notion of the self-made man was born—someone who started with nothing but rose to prominence and fortune through their own hard work, ingenuity, and sheer determination.

This narrative has remained a dominant part of the American ethos. Throughout the 20th century, and into the 21st century, figures like Andrew Carnegie, John D. Rockefeller, and J.P. Morgan were revered as the heroes of the American story. Their success stories were held up as models for others to follow. Today, people still reference their examples to illustrate the potential for success in America, whether in business, tech, or entertainment.

The Gilded Age also cemented the idea that financial success was the ultimate measure of achievement. While wealth had always been important in America, the sheer scale of wealth accumulated during this period made it clear that those who could amass fortunes on the order of Carnegie's steel empire or Rockefeller's oil monopoly were the true leaders of society. This idea—that financial wealth is a legitimate form of social power and influence—endured long after the Gilded Age ended. Today, we still see this sentiment echoed in the prominence of billionaires who shape everything from politics to culture.

Another enduring legacy of the Gilded Age is the deep-seated fascination with luxury. The wealthy of the late 19th century lived lives of opulence and spectacle—mansions, designer fashion, fine art, and lavish parties were common features of their daily existence. This culture of excess wasn't just about enjoying wealth in private; it was about putting it on display for everyone to see. Today, this has evolved into the celebrity culture and social media presence that surrounds modern-day billionaires and high-net-worth individuals. Figures like Elon Musk, Jeff Bezos, and Kylie Jenner are just the latest in a long line of individuals who have leveraged their wealth to become icons of success and influence, much like their Gilded Age predecessors.

The original Gilded Age also reinforced the idea that wealth was something to be celebrated and flaunted. In today's world, that legacy has evolved into an entire industry built around the display of wealth. From luxury brands to social media influencers to real estate moguls showcasing their homes in magazines and online, the obsession with showing off wealth is perhaps one of the most enduring aspects of the Gilded Age's cultural legacy. The values of the Gilded Age, built around the pursuit of luxury, status, and social power, are reflected in today's culture more than ever.

## The Gilded Age Reborn?

So, is the Gilded Age reborn? It's a question worth asking as we look at today's world of billionaires, tech moguls, and the media-driven cult of wealth. While the original Gilded Age may have ended in the early 20th century, the forces that shaped it—capitalism, entrepreneurial ambition, consumerism, and the celebration of excess—have only intensified in the 21st century.

Take a look at the world of Silicon Valley, where tech billionaires like Mark Zuckerberg, Elon Musk, and Larry Page have become the new financial titans of the modern era. Just as the industrialists of the Gilded Age transformed their industries and reshaped the American economy, these modern moguls have revolutionized technology, social media, and space exploration. Their wealth has reached levels that were once unimaginable, creating a new breed of celebrity entrepreneurs whose names are as well-known as those of the Gilded Age industrialists.

Today's elite, much like their 19th-century counterparts, are public figures whose lives are scrutinized, dissected, and idolized by the media. Social media, in particular, has become the modern-day equivalent of the society columns of the Gilded Age, where the lives of the rich and famous are chronicled for the world to see. From private jets to luxury yachts, billionaires are constantly documenting their opulent lifestyles, ensuring their wealth and success are on full display. The sense of fascination with wealth that defined the original Gilded Age is still very much alive and well today, albeit in a new form.

Moreover, the pursuit of wealth has once again become central to the American Dream. While the idea of the self-made man originated in the Gilded Age, it has only grown more prominent in today's culture. The new icons of wealth, whether in tech, finance, or entertainment, continue to promote the idea that anyone, regardless of their background, can achieve massive success if they have the right combination of ideas, ambition, and drive. The rise of digital entrepreneurs, online influencers, and the growing wealth inequality only underscore the reality that today's version of the American Dream is still heavily rooted in the pursuit of wealth and social status.

But unlike the Gilded Age, the current era is more complicated. Wealth today is no longer just about railroads and steel mills. It is about data, intellectual property, and tech innovation. This shift has made wealth creation more accessible to people from diverse backgrounds, but it has also exacerbated the wealth gap, creating a new cultural divide between the ultra-wealthy and the rest of society.

As we continue to move through the 21st century, we will see how these themes—the pursuit of wealth, the culture of excess, and the celebration of success—continue to unfold. The Gilded Revival that we are experiencing today is more than just a return to opulence—it is a reimagining of the original Gilded Age, shaped by new technologies, new industries, and new cultural forces. Whether this new era will be as transformative and enduring as the first remains to be seen.

## Conclusion

In the chapters to follow, we will explore how the Gilded Revival is playing out in today's world. We will examine the ways in which wealth, luxury, and success are manifesting in the 21st century, from the rise of billionaire tech moguls to the increasing visibility of luxury lifestyles on social media. We will also look at the cultural impact of this new era, asking whether we are witnessing a resurgence of the values that defined the first Gilded Age—or whether something new is emerging. What is clear is that, just as in the past, wealth and its accompanying symbols of success will continue to shape the American identity for generations to come.

# Shifting Cultural Attitudes Toward Wealth

The allure of wealth has always been a central element of the American Dream, but over the course of the past century, the attitudes toward wealth and its role in society have undergone significant transformation. From the early days of industrialization to the rise of consumer culture, the way Americans view financial success and luxury has shifted, creating a complex relationship between aspiration, status, and values.

As we look around today, we can see that the idea of wealth is not just about material gain or economic power; it's also deeply intertwined with the way we define success, personal achievement, and social standing. But how did we get here? How did the American obsession with wealth evolve from the humble beginnings of the colonial economy to the glittering world of tech moguls, social media influencers, and luxury lifestyles?

In this chapter, we will trace the evolution of cultural attitudes toward wealth, looking at the shifting perceptions of what it means to be wealthy, successful, and powerful. We will examine the role that society, media, and politics have played in reshaping these views and how these changes have influenced both the elite class and the average citizen.

The first major shift occurred with the Industrial Revolution and the rise of the first billionaires, where wealth was increasingly seen as a sign of accomplishment, ingenuity, and hard work. This period, dominated by men like Andrew Carnegie and John D. Rockefeller, set the stage for the cultural ideal of the self-made man, an archetype that became central to American identity. Wealth was no longer something that came from aristocratic lineage or inheritance; it was something that could be earned—through vision, risk-taking, and relentless ambition.

Then came the Gilded Age, an era where wealth was flaunted and displayed like never before. The elite class built palatial homes, hosted extravagant parties, and dressed in the finest fashion, all while creating a new culture of glamour that would become ingrained in American society. However, as we all know, the public's adulation of the wealthy was tempered by the rise of populist movements and criticism of excess, which sparked the first real debates about the moral responsibility of wealth.

Fast-forward to the 20th century, and wealth continued to play a central role in shaping American values. But as Hollywood, the media, and the advertising industry rose to prominence, wealth began to be marketed not just as a symbol of success, but also as a lifestyle—one to be emulated and admired. This era saw the rise of celebrity culture, with wealthy actors, musicians, and business moguls influencing everything from fashion to politics. At the same time, the rise of the middle class and the expansion of consumerism led to a shift in how ordinary Americans viewed their own wealth aspirations.

By the turn of the 21st century, we saw the democratization of wealth, thanks to the internet, social media, and the rise of the sharing economy. Suddenly, wealth wasn't just for the ultra-rich; it was something that could be aspired to by anyone with a good idea, a large following, or the right amount of luck. Tech billionaires, startups, and influencers began to rewrite the rules of what it meant to be successful, offering up new models of wealth that were not based on traditional industries but instead on innovation, creativity, and personal branding.

In this chapter, we will look closely at these shifts, exploring how attitudes toward wealth have evolved and the impact this has had on everything from social mobility to national identity. We will also consider the future of wealth in America, asking whether the rise of new wealth creators, fueled by technology and globalization, will continue to reshape our cultural values or whether new challenges—like economic inequality and ethical concerns—will push us to reconsider the role that wealth should play in society.

Ultimately, this chapter is about understanding the cultural currents that have shaped the American obsession with wealth, and how they continue to influence the way we live, work, and think about success today. From the Gilded Age to the digital revolution, wealth has not only been a source of power and influence, but also a symbol of the ideals we hold dear—ingenuity, ambition, and the promise of a brighter future.

## From Gold Rush to Glitter: The Evolution of Wealth in America

As we dive deeper into the evolution of America's relationship with wealth, it's crucial to understand how wealth was viewed in the earliest days of the nation's history. In the early 19th century, much of American wealth came from land and agriculture. The land-owning elite in places like Virginia and New England were seen as the country's first aristocrats, though they were often far more modest than their European counterparts. They controlled much of the land and, in turn, the economic power of the nation. However, economic mobility was still limited. For many, the path to wealth was blocked by the class system and a relatively rigid social structure.

The Industrial Revolution, however, began to change all that. With the advent of factories, railroads, and mass production, new opportunities for wealth creation emerged. Men like Andrew Carnegie, John D.

Rockefeller, and Cornelius Vanderbilt weren't born into wealth. Instead, they built empires from the ground up, becoming the first truly self-made millionaires of America. Their stories became the blueprint for the American Dream, showing the country that anyone, no matter their background, could amass great wealth with enough drive, vision, and determination.

The late 19th century was a time of extraordinary economic growth. However, it was also a time of great contrast. While the elite were amassing vast fortunes, the working class struggled to make ends meet. The disparity between the ultra-wealthy and the poor was stark, leading to debates about economic inequality that still echo in today's political discourse.

## The Gilded Age: Opulence and Backlash

By the Gilded Age, the focus on wealth had reached its peak. The newly rich elite sought to outdo one another with palatial estates, lavish balls, and public displays of wealth. This was a time of excess, where the pursuit of luxury became the standard of success. Alva Vanderbilt, Caroline Astor, and other socialites became household names, with their lives chronicled in the press, their clothes admired, and their parties imitated by those who aspired to their lifestyle.

But with the excess came a growing sense of discontent. As the wealth gap continued to widen, so did the calls for reform. The rise of populism, labor movements, and social justice signaled that not everyone viewed the wealthy elite as the symbols of American success. For many, the new wealth epitomized everything that was wrong with society: the concentration of power in the hands of a few, the exploitation of workers, and the lack of accountability among the ultra-rich.

## The Rise of Celebrity Culture and the Birth of Wealth Icons

As we moved into the 20th century, the relationship between wealth and celebrity became even more pronounced. The rise of Hollywood, the expansion of media, and the advertising industry turned wealth into something to be admired and, in many cases, aspired to. Actors, musicians, and sports stars became the new icons of wealth, their names and images plastered on magazines, billboards, and television screens across the world. Wealth was no longer just about industry; it was about lifestyle—about luxury, fashion, and the ability to live a life that ordinary people could only dream of.

The celebrity culture of the mid-20th century laid the foundation for today's social media-driven wealth. Figures like Elvis Presley, Marilyn Monroe, and Frank Sinatra were among the first to build their personal brands and turn their wealth into something aspirational. Today, this phenomenon is even more pronounced, with the rise of influencers, YouTubers, and Instagram stars who have made luxury a part of their online identity. These individuals, while not always from traditional industries like finance or entertainment, have become some of the most visible and influential figures in today's culture of wealth.

## Conclusion: The Future of Wealth in America

As we conclude this chapter, we have seen how attitudes toward wealth have shifted from the early days of America to the modern era. From the Gilded Age to the celebrity-driven wealth culture of today, the concept of what it means to be wealthy has undergone significant changes. These shifts are reflective of a larger transformation in American culture, in which wealth and success have become deeply intertwined with our ideas of personal achievement, identity, and aspiration.

As we move further into the 21st century, the question remains: will these evolving attitudes continue to shape the future of wealth in

America, or will new forces—economic inequality, political change, and ethical concerns—force us to reevaluate the role of wealth in our lives?

This chapter sets the stage for a deeper exploration of how wealth has become a cultural force, and how it will continue to impact society, economics, and values in the years to come.

## Chapter 2.1: The 1980s – The Return of Wealth as Status

The 1980s in America were a time of radical cultural transformation, fueled by economic policies, a booming stock market, and an undeniable shift in societal values. It was an era marked by the reemergence of wealth as a powerful symbol of success, status, and personal achievement. The cultural fabric of the decade was heavily influenced by the economic climate under the Reagan administration, which championed tax cuts, deregulation, and an aggressive push for free-market capitalism. These policies set the stage for a new form of American opulence, one that wasn't just about affluence but about displaying it boldly, unapologetically, and above all—exclusively.

For many, the 1980s represented a kind of financial renaissance, where wealth was not only attainable but something to be celebrated and flaunted. It was a period that saw the rebirth of the American Dream—except this time, the dream was more materialistic, focused on the accumulation of possessions, luxury goods, and the outward display of affluence. And no group epitomized this cultural shift better than the Yuppies—the young urban professionals who made up the heart of the decade's wealth-obsessed ethos.

As the Stock Market boomed, and Wall Street became a symbol of financial power, the iconic figure of the corporate raider emerged, alongside greed-fueled ambition that would later be immortalized in pop culture. The decade produced the rise of wealth fetishism, where excess wasn't just tolerated—it was encouraged, glamorized, and immortalized in film, music, and media. In this chapter, we'll explore how these forces shaped the 1980s as the decade when wealth as status came roaring back, a defining moment that still reverberates in America's obsession with luxury and financial success today.

## The Reagan Era and a Cultural Shift

When Ronald Reagan took office in 1981, America was on the brink of economic change. The country had just come through a challenging period of stagflation, and an energy crisis that left many Americans feeling uncertain about the future. Reagan, who had campaigned on a promise to reinvigorate the American economy, implemented a series of economic policies designed to stimulate growth and reduce government intervention in business.

Reagan's tax cuts were among the most significant elements of his economic agenda. By slashing income taxes for individuals and corporations, the Reagan administration believed it could foster a more entrepreneurial environment, one where people would have greater incentives to invest and expand businesses. At the same time, Reagan pushed for deregulation in industries ranging from banking to telecommunications, removing many of the restraints that had limited corporate expansion in the previous decades. For the first time in years, there was a real sense of economic optimism and the belief that financial success was not just a possibility—it was an expectation.

This period marked a sharp cultural shift, with the aspiration for wealth moving to the forefront of the American consciousness. Materialism began to be seen as an indicator of success, and those who were able to display their financial achievements openly were admired, even revered. This shift was bolstered by the media, which began to glorify the wealthy elite, turning them into cultural icons. High-rise offices in the Wall Street district, mansions in Beverly Hills, and luxury cars became symbols of the new ideal. The American Dream was no longer just about owning a home or achieving personal freedom—it was about making money and showing the world how successful you had become.

The Reagan-era policies, coupled with the booming stock market, helped to create a class of wealthy individuals who embodied the decade's values. Business tycoons and corporate moguls emerged as the new heroes of American society. Figures like Donald Trump, Ross Perot, and Ivan Boesky became larger-than-life personas, with their wealth and ambition making them household names. But it wasn't just about entrepreneurs; corporate executives were also enjoying unprecedented salaries and bonuses, cementing their place in the social stratosphere. Greed wasn't just accepted; it was embraced as a driving force behind economic success.

## The Rise of the "Yuppie"

If the 1980s had a mascot for the pursuit of wealth, it would undoubtedly be the Yuppie. This term, short for young urban professional, quickly became a cultural phenomenon, representing a new generation that was enthusiastic about wealth, luxury, and status symbols. Yuppies were typically in their 20s or 30s, well-educated, and highly ambitious, striving to climb the corporate ladder and live the high life. They gravitated toward metropolitan centers, especially cities like New York, Los Angeles, and Chicago, where they could showcase their success in the form of designer clothes, sports cars, and exclusive social circles.

The Yuppie ideal was all about outward displays of wealth and success, encapsulating the notion that "you are what you own". They were the first generation to truly embrace the idea of status symbols as markers of identity. Their lifestyle was marked by a constant desire for the best of everything: the latest gadgets, the most exclusive restaurants, the most fashionable apparel, and the most luxurious apartments. In short, Yuppies didn't just want wealth—they wanted to flaunt it.

A key part of the Yuppie phenomenon was their relationship with consumerism. The economic environment of the Reagan years encouraged individuals to spend freely, particularly on luxury items. Personal credit was becoming more accessible, and the growing financial markets allowed many to invest their wealth with confidence. The idea that one could spend money to prove one's worth became central to the Yuppie lifestyle.

Cultural markers, such as the Montblanc pen, the Rolex watch, and Italian leather shoes, became associated with success. The Yuppie was the first generation to truly embrace branded identity, where the logos of high-end goods were displayed as a way of declaring, "I have arrived." These displays weren't just about function; they were about aesthetic power, signaling that the wearer had the financial wherewithal to participate in the exclusive world of the elite. The Yuppie aesthetic was all about polish, precision, and an unmistakable aura of success.

## Wall Street and Wealth Fetishism

No other symbol from the 1980s better encapsulates the rise of wealth as status than the Wall Street ethos, which was crystallized in the 1987 film Wall Street, directed by Oliver Stone. The movie's central character, Gordon Gekko, portrayed by Michael Douglas, became the embodiment of 1980s financial greed. His infamous line, "Greed is good," became a rallying cry for a generation that viewed unfettered capitalism as a path to unlimited success.

Wall Street depicted a world where wealth was not just a result of hard work or smart investment, but rather a product of ruthless ambition and a willingness to do whatever it took to secure financial dominance. The film celebrated the corporate raider mentality, where high-stakes investments, hostile takeovers, and insider trading were seen as acceptable tactics for achieving financial success. Gekko's character, with his tailored suits, private jets, and luxurious lifestyle, became an ideal for many young professionals who admired his confidence and unapologetic pursuit of wealth.

The influence of Wall Street cannot be overstated. The film became a cultural touchstone, helping to shape the way Americans viewed wealth in the 1980s. The idea of wealth as a competitive sport took hold, where financial triumphs were seen as personal victories. Gekko's motto of "Greed is good" became more than just a line from a movie; it encapsulated a decade-long shift in how Americans thought about money and its role in society. It became cool to be rich, and the pursuit of financial success was no longer something to be whispered about in boardrooms; it was something to be celebrated, flaunted, and glorified.

## Conclusion

The 1980s marked the return of wealth as status in America, facilitated by Reagan-era economic policies, the rise of the Yuppie culture, and the embrace of greed and excess as ideals. The combination of tax cuts, deregulation, and a thriving stock market created the perfect environment for financial optimism to thrive. The decade's fixation on luxury, fashion, and wealth became a national obsession, one that left a lasting imprint on American society.

As we continue to see in the 21st century, the 1980s helped to establish the foundation for today's consumer culture, where wealth is not just a sign of economic success but also an expression of identity. The influence of the Reagan years, the rise of the Yuppie, and the celebration of wealth in Wall Street can still be seen today in the relentless pursuit of luxury, success, and status that defines much of modern America.

In the next chapter, we will explore how this cultural obsession with wealth evolved in the decades that followed, and how it continues to shape the American identity and societal values around money, success, and status.

# Chapter 2.2: The Dot-Com Boom and the Redefinition of Success

The 1990s were a transformative decade in the landscape of American wealth, with the dot-com boom marking one of the most significant cultural and economic shifts in modern history. As the internet emerged as the backbone of a new digital age, a new breed of entrepreneurs began to accumulate vast fortunes through innovation rather than traditional industries like manufacturing, banking, or oil. The Silicon Valley revolution reshaped not only the way businesses were conducted but also how success, ambition, and wealth were perceived in American society.

In this chapter, we explore the rise of Silicon Valley as the epicenter of a new kind of wealth—a wealth defined by ideas, technology, and disruption. This new wave of wealthy individuals were not just corporate magnates; they were visionaries who gained fortune by transforming industries, creating startups that defied traditional business models, and building companies that changed the very fabric of modern life.

In parallel, the dot-com entrepreneurs introduced a new image of wealth—one that was less concerned with outward displays of luxury and more focused on the spirit of innovation and lifestyle choices. Where the 1980s yuppies had flaunted their success with designer labels and luxurious possessions, the new tech moguls reveled in a more casual, anti-elite approach. Hoodies and jeans replaced suits and ties, and wealth was symbolized less by opulent personal brands and more by the ability to disrupt markets and lead digital startups.

At the same time, the millennial generation, coming of age during the tech boom, began to see wealth in a new light. For them, financial success was no longer about corporate ladders or inherited fortunes; it was about creating something new, something that could revolutionize industries and change the world. The tech boom not only altered the course of American business but also redefined the very meaning of financial success—and this would leave a lasting impact on how wealth is viewed in the 21st century.

## The Technology Revolution

The late 1990s saw the rise of the dot-com bubble, a period when the world of technology and entrepreneurship converged, giving birth to a new generation of wealth creators. Silicon Valley, the tech hub nestled in Northern California, became the heart of this revolution, fostering startups that would grow into some of the largest and most influential companies in the world. Companies like Amazon, Google, eBay, and Yahoo weren't just businesses—they were global empires being built from the ground up, often by young entrepreneurs in their 20s and 30s who had little more than big ideas and ambition.

Before the 1990s, traditional industries like manufacturing, oil, and banking were the main drivers of American wealth. Tycoons like John D. Rockefeller, Andrew Carnegie, and J.P. Morgan had set the standard for financial success, amassing their fortunes in heavy industries. The world they inhabited was one of opulence, but also one that was rooted in the physical—the oil fields, the steel mills, the railroads. But in the 1990s, a new breed of entrepreneur began to rise—a breed who built their fortunes on software, hardware, and the emerging internet economy.

The internet became the primary vehicle for these new entrepreneurs. It opened up global markets in a way that traditional industries never could. Silicon Valley became a magnet for young, ambitious individuals with big ideas about how to leverage this new technology to transform business, commerce, and society itself. At the heart of this movement were the likes of Jeff Bezos, who founded Amazon in 1994; Larry Page and Sergey Brin, who created Google in 1998; and Pierre Omidyar, who launched eBay in 1995. These individuals were not inheritors of vast family fortunes—they were self-made billionaires, driven by their vision of what the world could look like when powered by the internet.

For the first time in history, it seemed possible to amass wealth not through physical resources or industrial production but through ideas, technology, and digital infrastructure. The rise of these new companies wasn't just about making money; it was about creating something revolutionary, something that could change the way the world operated. The tech moguls of the 1990s were not only wealthy—they were visionaries, and their companies were reshaping the global economy.

The dot-com boom created a sense of endless possibilities, where young entrepreneurs could become billionaires almost overnight. Unlike the earlier industrialists who built their fortunes through the hard work of mining, steel, or oil, the new Silicon Valley entrepreneurs were building their wealth from zeroes and ones—lines of code, digital platforms, and consumer innovations. The internet wasn't just an emerging market; it was an entirely new frontier, and those who could stake a claim early would reap the rewards.

## Casual Wealth and the "Anti-Elite" Elite

One of the most notable aspects of the dot-com era was the way that the image of wealth was fundamentally redefined. In the 1980s, the wealthy were often associated with high-end fashion, luxury cars, and prestige. Wealth was symbolized by the bling, the brash displays of opulence, and the luxury brands that became synonymous with success. But the tech moguls of the 1990s didn't need to dress in tailored suits or drive Ferraris to prove their success. In fact, many of them were deliberately rejecting the norms of the old-money elite in favor of a more casual, understated approach to wealth.

Where the yuppies of the 1980s had used luxury items as a way to advertise their success, the dot-com entrepreneurs found other ways to show their wealth. For many of these individuals, luxury brands and status symbols felt out of place. Instead, they embraced a more casual, comfortable style—jeans, t-shirts, and hoodies became the uniform of the new elite. The Silicon Valley look was often centered around minimalism and functionality rather than flashiness and excess.

This shift wasn't just about fashion; it was about the culture of Silicon Valley itself. The tech moguls of the 1990s—Steve Jobs, Mark Zuckerberg, Bill Gates, and others—cultivated a sense of being down-to-earth and anti-elite, even as their personal fortunes swelled into the billions. Jobs, for example, was known for wearing his signature black turtleneck, jeans, and sneakers—a far cry from the Armani suits worn by the financial moguls of Wall Street. The message was clear: wealth didn't need to be flashy or excessive to be real.

This anti-elite elite broke with the traditions of earlier wealthy classes. Instead of showcasing wealth through material symbols, they flaunted their entrepreneurial success and innovation. It wasn't about what you owned; it was about what you had created and the impact your work could have on the world.

For this new generation of wealth creators, the true measure of success was the ability to disrupt existing industries, to build businesses that could change the way the world worked. The goal was no longer just to acquire wealth—it was to innovate, reinvent, and transform. The tech moguls of the 1990s had a different vision of success—one that was defined not by material accumulation but by the power to change the world through technology.

## Changing Aspirations Among Millennials

The impact of the dot-com boom wasn't limited to Silicon Valley. It also had a profound effect on the generation that came of age during the tech explosion: Millennials. For many young people growing up in the 1990s and early 2000s, the idea that wealth could be achieved through entrepreneurship and technology was both aspirational and attainable. Unlike earlier generations, who viewed success through the lens of traditional career paths—such as law, finance, or medicine—millennials began to see the potential for wealth creation in industries that didn't exist when their parents were growing up.

As a result, the Millennial mindset was shaped by the idea that entrepreneurship and innovation could lead to incredible wealth. The tech industry wasn't just a career path—it was a place where anyone, with the right idea and a bit of luck, could make a fortune. Bill Gates, Mark Zuckerberg, Evan Spiegel, and Jack Dorsey were living proof that success didn't have to come from traditional means. It could come from creating an app, building a website, or disrupting an industry with a new idea.

This entrepreneurial mindset fueled a generation of millennials who were not content with simply climbing the corporate ladder. They were inspired to build their own ladders, to create companies and products that could redefine industries and shape the future. As the tech industry boomed, so did the aspirations of millennials. They no longer saw wealth as something inherited or passed down through family lines. Instead, they saw it as something that could be earned through creativity, drive, and innovation.

As the world entered the 21st century, millennials were coming of age with a new vision of what success and wealth could be—one that was shaped by the incredible possibilities of the digital age. And as they entered the workforce, they began to reshape the very concept of what it meant to be wealthy in America. The dot-com boom had not only created new fortunes—it had redefined the American Dream.

As we move forward, we'll look at how this new generation's values and aspirations continue to influence the way wealth is pursued, celebrated, and achieved today.

# Chapter 2.3: The Rebirth of Wealth Aspiration in the 2020s

In the early years of the 2020s, something fascinating occurred. Wealth and the aspiration to attain it came back into the cultural spotlight with a vigor and urgency unseen since the golden days of the Gilded Age or the brashness of the 1980s financial boom. But this time, the vehicle of aspiration wasn't Wall Street or Silicon Valley; it was the ever-present, always-connected world of social media. As Instagram, TikTok, and YouTube became dominant forces, wealth wasn't something people just read about in newspapers or saw in movies—it became a living, breathing reality, streamed into our lives in real-time, on-demand. Influencers and entrepreneurs became not just symbols of wealth but representatives of a new, more accessible path to financial success and luxury.

The visual nature of social media enabled wealth and luxury to be displayed in ways that were both immediate and constant. Exotic travels, private jets, luxury homes, and even day-to-day purchases became staples of a digital culture that redefined what it meant to be successful. At the same time, a generation of self-made moguls—some celebrities, some not—took center stage, their entrepreneurial journeys and the resulting wealth broadcasted to millions. We will now explore how the 2020s have reignited society's obsession with wealth, how social media has played a leading role in this rebirth, and how experiential luxury has emerged as the new definition of glamour.

## The Influence of Social Media on Wealth Perception

It's no secret that social media has fundamentally transformed the way we experience the world. From Facebook and Instagram to TikTok, these platforms are no longer just places for social connection or entertainment. They've become crucial vehicles for how we present ourselves, our lifestyles, and how we consume what others are doing. And for millennials and Generation Z, social media is the lens through which they view success, wealth, and even the American Dream.

The impact of social media on the perception of wealth cannot be overstated. Platforms like Instagram have inundated our feeds with images of luxury—from private islands to designer clothes, from luxurious spa treatments to high-end cars. Influencers, celebrities, and entrepreneurs post daily content that showcases a life of abundance. The result? Wealth is no longer a distant concept, accessible only to the elite. It is visible, tangible, and, perhaps most importantly, attainable for those with the right skills, drive, and visibility.

Take Instagram, for example, where curated lifestyle posts dominate feeds. Wealth is not simply about having a lavish home or exotic vacations; it's about showing it off in a way that sparks envy and inspiration. Hashtags like #wealth, #luxurylifestyle, and #entrepreneur generate millions of posts, each depicting a carefully constructed image of success. The aesthetic of wealth has become so important that influencers and celebrities dedicate hours to creating the perfect shot, one that conveys not just luxury but an entire lifestyle.

TikTok, with its rapid-fire, viral content, has taken this trend to new heights. Short, snappy videos show wealth and success in real time—whether it's an influencer unboxing an expensive purchase, a behind-the-scenes look at a millionaire's lifestyle, or a glamorous overseas vacation. The rapid dissemination of content means that wealth is front and center in a way that was previously impossible.

Even YouTube—the birthplace of the vlog—has become a space where wealth and success are showcased in an even more personal, accessible way. Creators give audiences a peek into their world, showing everything from their luxurious homes to the products they use to their entrepreneurial endeavors. While in the past, wealth was something to be admired from afar, social media has transformed it into something that feels attainable, not just through traditional career routes but through the power of branding, content creation, and entrepreneurship.

Thus, social media has had a two-fold impact on perceptions of wealth: it has not only made wealth more visible and accessible but also democratized it. Where wealth was once an exclusive affair of the elite, today's digital influencers and entrepreneurs show that financial success can be achieved by anyone with a strong personal brand, a following, and an innovative idea. These new icons of wealth aren't just born into their riches—they've built them.

## The Rise of Personal Branding and "Self-Made" Wealth

Perhaps the most significant shift in how wealth is understood today is the rise of the self-made millionaire—an image that has been championed by social media moguls like Kylie Jenner, Elon Musk, and Mark Zuckerberg, and has been heralded as the new ideal for wealth accumulation. Unlike the industrial titans of the past, who amassed fortunes through legacy industries, today's wealth creators have built their empires on the power of personal branding and entrepreneurial innovation.

Let's start with Kylie Jenner. A name synonymous with the self-made billionaire label, Kylie gained attention with her beauty brand, Kylie Cosmetics. What made her rise so extraordinary wasn't just the products themselves, but the fact that she was able to leverage her personal brand—built through years of social media visibility and reality TV fame—into a global empire. Jenner became the epitome of the self-made mogul, using her platform to promote her products to millions of followers, creating a brand that felt authentic and relatable, even as it raked in hundreds of millions of dollars.

Similarly, Elon Musk has reinvented the idea of what it means to be a self-made billionaire. The CEO of Tesla and SpaceX, Musk has used his social media presence—particularly Twitter—to cultivate a reputation as a tech innovator and futurist. His public persona has become inseparable from the success of his companies. Musk's personal narrative—from his humble beginnings in South Africa to his rise as one of the world's most influential entrepreneurs—has played a massive role in both shaping his brand and making his wealth seem achievable for those who think outside the box.

Then there's Mark Zuckerberg, whose journey from Harvard dorm rooms to the founder of Facebook embodies the modern American Dream. Zuckerberg's path to wealth has been deeply intertwined with his digital persona. His role as both a creator and a public figure has allowed him to use his own story to captivate millions around the world. His success—like Musk and Jenner's—reminds people that wealth can be earned by creating something innovative, and with the right visibility, it can turn into something global.

For many young people in the 2020s, these entrepreneurs have become the embodiment of the new American Dream—one that doesn't require wealthy parents, prestigious education, or old-school connections. Instead, it's about building a personal brand, growing a following, and creating a business from scratch.

This is a major departure from traditional wealth accumulation methods. The idea that you could be wealthy through digital content, social media presence, or personal brand building is a defining characteristic of wealth in the 21st century. Social media has allowed millennials and Generation Z to view wealth not as something inherited or passed down but as something that can be created on your own terms.

## Experiential Luxury and the Modern Definition of Glamour

Where the Gilded Age elite flaunted their fortunes through grand material possessions—from mansions to jewels—today's wealthy are increasingly emphasizing experiences over material goods. This shift is perhaps best encapsulated in the rise of experiential luxury—a new way of defining and showcasing wealth that places emphasis on exclusive experiences rather than tangible possessions.

In the 2020s, luxury is no longer just about owning the latest sports car or private yacht. It's about having access to bespoke services—whether it's a private tour of art museums in Paris or a weekend retreat in a private island in the Maldives. Luxury travel is at the forefront of this movement. The idea of the luxury experience is about being in extraordinary places, doing extraordinary things, and having memories rather than items to show for it.

For example, consider the rising trend of wellness tourism. The wealthy in the 2020s are often seeking high-end health retreats, private fitness classes, and even spiritual journeys to far-flung locations. Similarly, exclusive dining experiences—from private chefs to fine-dining pop-ups in unexpected locations—have become a hallmark of the new luxury.

Today's wealth is about experiences that are uniquely shareable—moments that can be broadcasted to millions of followers, making them part of a digital narrative. Instagram, for instance, has become the ultimate showcase for these kinds of experiences. Wealth is often about having access to places and moments that others can only dream of, and the ability to share those moments with an eager, aspirational audience.

It's clear that wealth aspiration in the 2020s is no longer just about acquiring things. It's about crafting a lifestyle, building a brand, and experiencing the extraordinary. The shift from materialism to experiential luxury speaks volumes about the changing face of wealth in the digital age, where what's valuable isn't always something you can hold in your hand—it's something you can share with the world.

In the next chapters, we'll dive deeper into the specific wealth icons and cultural shifts driving this transformation. From influencers to entrepreneurs, we'll explore how these individuals are shaping the new gilded age of wealth and glamour.

# Chapter 2.4: From Modesty to Magnificence: A Full Circle Return to Wealth Glamour

In the course of American history, wealth has always been a topic that teeters between being openly flaunted and quietly accumulated. From the opulent displays of the Gilded Age to the more restrained and conservative post-World War II era, and the Yuppie-fueled 1980s, America's relationship with wealth has always been a reflection of its broader social, economic, and cultural shifts. But as we moved into the 2020s, something remarkable happened—a full-circle return to the celebration of wealth and glamour. Today, wealth is no longer hidden behind closed doors or downplayed in the name of modesty. It is once again front and center, made visible and tangible through the lens of social media, entrepreneurship, and globalization.

In this chapter, we will explore how America has once again embraced the ideals of wealth, luxury, and financial aspiration, heralding a "Gilded Revival". This modern era is not just a return to old-world glamour but a reimagining of it—blending the timeless allure of opulence with the innovative drive of today's most influential industries. The wealth of today is no longer defined by the same symbols of affluence as in the past, but the aspiration to achieve it has never been stronger.

## A New Era of Financial Openness

The shift back to financial openness is perhaps most clearly visible through the lens of social media. In past decades, wealth was often a private affair—those who had it kept it behind closed doors, building fortunes in quiet industries like finance, real estate, and manufacturing. But the 2020s have seen a dramatic shift. Now, wealth is not something to be kept hidden but something to be flaunted and celebrated. The rise of platforms like Instagram, TikTok, and YouTube has transformed the way people interact with wealth. These platforms have given ordinary people a window into the lives of the wealthy, while also offering new avenues for the wealthy to display their success and luxury in ways that were previously unimaginable.

Today, it's not unusual for influencers, entrepreneurs, and even celebrities to showcase their wealth on a daily basis, turning their luxurious lifestyles into content for millions of followers. Whether it's posting pictures of private jets, showing off the latest designer clothes, or offering glimpses of vacations in exotic locales, social media has made wealth more visible than ever before.

This openness is not just about showing wealth but also about embracing it as a cultural value. Whereas, in past decades, there was often a sense of guilt or modesty surrounding wealth—the idea that flaunting it was in bad taste or morally questionable—today, there's a much more open, unapologetic embrace of financial success. It is no longer about simply "making it"; it is about celebrating it, owning it, and creating a brand around it. The stories of self-made billionaires like Kylie Jenner, Elon Musk, and Jeff Bezos—who rose from modest beginnings to dominate their respective industries—are shared and celebrated on social media, creating new role models and providing the narrative that anyone can achieve the same level of success.

In fact, the shift toward financial openness is not just a passing trend but a reflection of broader societal values. Wealth, in this new context, is not seen as a source of shame but as a goal—one that people are encouraged to work toward, and one that can be achieved through the right combination of talent, innovation, and visibility. This embrace of wealth as something to aspire to is perhaps the most striking characteristic of today's modern Gilded Revival.

## From Modesty to Magnificence: A Return to Glamour

While financial openness is a key factor in this new era of wealth, it's the return to glamour that truly distinguishes the current period from the past. The Gilded Age was synonymous with magnificent displays of wealth—grand mansions, extravagant parties, designer clothes, and lavish entertaining. The ultra-wealthy of that time made sure their wealth was not only evident to those around them but was also deeply ingrained in the culture. Wealth was not simply a personal achievement; it was a public statement.

Today's wealthy are embracing a similar approach to wealth and status. Luxury fashion, exotic travel, private experiences, and bespoke services have become the new symbols of success. The difference now, however, is that these symbols are constantly on display, as the line between personal life and brand-building becomes increasingly blurred. Wealth is not just a matter of owning material possessions; it's about curating a lifestyle that is both aspirational and accessible, one that can be shared with the world and celebrated by millions.

Take the rise of luxury travel, for example. While the ultra-wealthy of the past would often retreat to their private estates or escape to secluded corners of the world, today's wealthy are sharing these experiences with their followers. Instagram influencers in particular are known for showcasing their luxurious getaways—from private yachts in the Mediterranean to villas in the Swiss Alps. The goal is not just to enjoy these experiences but to show them off to a vast, adoring audience. In this way, wealth is not just for the individual's pleasure—it is also a tool for social capital.

Similarly, the focus on experiential luxury has redefined what glamour looks like in the 21st century. Rather than collecting things, today's wealthy are collecting memories—whether that's through once-in-a-lifetime travel experiences, exclusive access to events, or unique, tailored services. The idea of luxury has evolved. It is no longer just about having more stuff than anyone else; it is about curating an experience that others can admire and even emulate.

## The Modern Gilded Revival: A New Kind of Wealth Icon

In today's Gilded Revival, wealth isn't just a measure of assets but a public display of personal achievement, influence, and accessibility. The new icons of wealth have redefined what it means to be affluent—not by inheriting riches but by building fortunes that are unmistakably visible and relatable. Just as the Vanderbilts, Rockefellers, and Carnegies once symbolized American ambition, today's wealth creators—like Taylor Swift, Emma Grede, and Jack Dorsey—embody a new American Dream, one where success is defined by innovation, personal branding, and a fearless approach to business.

One of the most compelling aspects of this modern era is how the boundaries between celebrity and entrepreneur have all but disappeared. Taylor Swift, for instance, didn't just stop at being one of the world's top musicians; she leveraged her influence to become one of the most profitable touring artists, making nearly $1 billion from her Eras Tour alone. Swift's meticulous control over her brand and ownership of her music catalog has turned her into a powerhouse not just in music but in finance and personal branding.

Emma Grede, co-founder of Good American and CEO of SKIMS, has also emerged as an influential figure who melds fashion with entrepreneurial prowess. By bringing inclusivity and body positivity into the mainstream, Grede's brands have resonated deeply with consumers, reshaping the fashion landscape and making her a prominent figure in business.

Then there's Jack Dorsey, who co-founded Twitter and Block (formerly Square) and has transformed digital communication and commerce in ways that reach people globally. Dorsey's ventures have pushed boundaries in both social media and fintech, turning him into a revered figure who connects technology with social change.

These modern wealth icons have redefined financial success by embracing visibility as much as achievement. Through social media, they've built personal brands that not only fuel their business interests but also cultivate an aspirational image that is relatable yet extraordinary. Today's wealthy figures don't just accumulate capital—they project a lifestyle, ethos, and sense of purpose that resonate on a cultural level. The new wealth of the 2020s, then, is not only about financial clout but about shaping conversations, influencing culture, and defining what it means to be aspirational in a way that feels accessible to millions.

## Setting the Stage for the Modern Gilded Age

As we look forward, it's clear that the new Gilded Age is here. And while it may look different from the Gilded Age of the 19th century, it is still fundamentally shaped by the same core principles—the pursuit of wealth, the desire for luxury, and the cultural fascination with success. In the coming chapters, we will explore the specific elements that are driving this new era of financial glamour—from social media to technological innovation and entrepreneurial ambition. We will look at how self-made billionaires and influencers are rewriting the rules of success, how experiential luxury is taking the place of materialism, and how America's cultural values are once again revolving around wealth, opulence, and achievement.

This modern era of financial aspiration is not just a passing trend; it is a reflection of shifting cultural norms and the deepening connection between wealth and identity. As we continue to navigate this new Gilded Revival, we'll witness how these forces shape not just the culture of the 2020s but the future of American ambition. This is a time when wealth is not just about accumulation—it's about identity, visibility, and the power of influence. The new age of financial glamour has only just begun.

# The Resurgence of Financial Glamour

We are living in an era where wealth is no longer just something to be accumulated in silence. It is something to be flaunted, displayed, and celebrated. From the glittering social media posts of influencers basking in the sun on private yachts to the opulent parties thrown by Silicon Valley moguls, today's wealth is ever-present and always in the spotlight. What was once hidden behind the closed doors of mansions, the quiet offices of bankers, and the private vaults of the ultra-rich has now exploded onto the public stage, where every detail is available for the world to see.

This marks the resurgence of financial glamour—a return to the opulence, extravagance, and larger-than-life displays of wealth that characterized the first Gilded Age in the late 19th century. However, unlike that earlier era, the resurgence of financial glamour today is not just about material displays. It is about the cultivation of identity, the rise of new icons, and the ability to control and shape the public narrative surrounding success.

In Part 2 of this book, we will explore how financial glamour is making a dramatic return in the 21st century. But this is not a simple repetition of the past. The forces driving today's resurgence of wealth—technology, media, entrepreneurship, and social media—are reshaping what it means to be rich and successful in the modern world. We live in a time where the traditional barriers to wealth creation—such as heritage, legacy, or even formal education—are no longer as important as visibility, innovation, and the ability to influence. The new icons of wealth are not just the heirs to industrial fortunes; they are the entrepreneurs, celebrities, and influencers who have created their wealth in the digital age, often without the traditional hallmarks of power that defined wealth in past generations.

This new era is driven by a powerful sense of individualism, where the idea of the self-made millionaire has never been more potent. With the rise of platforms like Instagram, YouTube, TikTok, and Twitter, anyone with a compelling story, a strong personal brand, and the right connections can find their path to financial success. These platforms have made it possible for entrepreneurs, entertainers, and even the everyday person to reach global audiences, turning personal wealth into something that is not just earned, but shared. Today's wealth is not merely a possession; it is part of a public identity, something to be flaunted, flaunted again, and then polished to a perfection that seems almost unattainable.

## The Role of Social Media in the Resurgence of Financial Glamour

The financial glamour of today is inseparable from the rise of social media. No longer are the stories of the rich confined to the pages of elite society magazines or whispered about in the corridors of power. Today, the everyday lives of the ultra-wealthy are constantly broadcast to millions of followers around the world, thanks to the growing influence of social platforms.

Social media has made wealth visible, accessible, and shareable. From Instagram influencers showcasing their jet-set lifestyles to YouTube millionaires documenting their rise to the top, social media has shifted the way we view the wealthy. In many ways, social media has democratized wealth, allowing those who are just starting out to follow the lives of their idols, see their paths to success, and potentially mimic them. But beyond mere visibility, social media has also changed the symbols of success themselves.

Examples run the gamut and include such individuals as:

## Alex Hormozi and the Rise of Accessible Wealth-Building Advice

Alex Hormozi, an entrepreneur and business educator, has amassed millions of followers on his YouTube and Instagram platforms by sharing his journey from gym owner to multi-million-dollar business advisor. His transparency about revenue numbers, investment strategies, and personal mistakes has turned him into a mentor for aspiring entrepreneurs. Rather than flaunting luxury items, Hormozi's content demystifies wealth-building by focusing on practical strategies anyone can implement, reshaping what financial success looks like online

He emphasizes the importance of authenticity and personal storytelling in building a brand through social media. "Your personal brand and your business's brand—they're not separate anymore." Hormozi believes that by inviting people into your journey and discussing aspects like your kids, spouse, and business, you can foster a supportive community.

## Emma Chamberlain and the Luxury Brand Influence

Emma Chamberlain, once known for her relatable, casual YouTube videos, has grown into a major influencer in the luxury fashion world. Her partnerships Louis Vuitton and Cartier, alongside her work at high-profile events such as the Met Gala, showcase a new kind of wealth icon—one who bridges casual, relatable content with luxury branding. Through her influence, Chamberlain has changed the symbols of success from overt displays of wealth to more subtle, personal, and experience-focused luxury.

## Grant Cardone's Accessible "10X" Lifestyle

Real estate mogul Grant Cardone has built a massive social media following by documenting his lavish lifestyle and sharing investment advice through YouTube, Instagram, and TikTok. His "10X" philosophy, which encourages extreme growth in both personal and financial realms, has become a guiding principle for many of his followers. Cardone's visibility on social media has made high-level real estate investment seem attainable and aspirational, encouraging followers to adopt similar approaches to wealth accumulation.

## MrBeast and the Evolution of Philanthropic Success

YouTube star MrBeast (Jimmy Donaldson) has revolutionized the way success is represented on social media by making philanthropy part of his brand. Through his videos, MrBeast donates large sums of money, gives away cars and homes, and funds large-scale charity projects. This approach has shifted symbols of success from just personal luxury to generosity and large-scale impact. His style appeals to young audiences and represents wealth as something that enables impactful, visible change.

## Chiara Ferragni and the Influence of Personal Branding in Fashion

Chiara Ferragni, a global fashion influencer and entrepreneur, turned her Instagram presence into a multimillion-dollar fashion empire. Starting with outfit-of-the-day posts, she built a massive following and eventually launched her own brand, The Blonde Salad, and a successful shoe line. Ferragni's visible journey from influencer to businesswoman exemplifies how wealth is now cultivated through personal brand-building, showing aspiring entrepreneurs how visibility and relatability can translate into financial success.

These examples illustrate how social media has not only made wealth more visible but has also democratized the concept of success, shifting it from exclusive luxury items to a focus on visibility, impact, and re-latability. Through social media, these icons of wealth have redefined success as something followers feel they can achieve in their own lives by replicating accessible, shareable paths to financial and personal goals.

In the past, wealth was often represented by tangible symbols: gold watches, mansions, expensive cars. Today, wealth is more likely to be represented by experiences—luxury vacations, private events, exotic foods, and exclusive access. The influencer economy is perhaps the most significant shift in this new era of financial glamour. Influencers are not just people with expensive tastes; they are creators who have built entire careers around the ability to influence their followers and sell an aspirational lifestyle. Their wealth is no longer just about possessions but the ability to cultivate and maintain an identity that millions of people want to buy into.

For example, these three influencers embody this transformation and have reached incredible levels of prominence in their respective fields

## Chiara Ferragni: The Fashion Icon with Global Reach

Chiara Ferragni, the Italian-born influencer behind *The Blonde Salad,* started out by simply sharing her outfits and style tips. But what began as a fashion blog evolved into a personal brand worth millions, turning Ferragni into a global fashion mogul. Chiara didn't just showcase products; she built a persona that people felt connected to and wanted to emulate. Today, Ferragni has her own fashion line, collaborations with brands like Louis Vuitton and Dior, and a social media following that puts her in the spotlight of every major fashion event. Her wealth isn't just about high-end clothing; it's about creating an exclusive lifestyle that her followers aspire to live, translating luxury fashion from high-end boutiques to an Instagram feed that anyone can follow.

## Gary Vaynerchuk: The Hustler Who Made Business Cool

Gary Vaynerchuk, commonly known as Gary Vee, isn't your typical influencer. He began with a YouTube channel documenting his journey of growing his family's wine business. Today, he's a digital marketing powerhouse and venture capitalist who shares his insights on business, branding, and entrepreneurship with millions of followers. What makes Gary unique is his raw, unfiltered approach; he openly discusses his failures, triumphs, and lessons in a way that resonates with people of all backgrounds. For Gary, wealth isn't about a high-rise penthouse or fancy cars but about the hustle, grind, and practical advice on making things happen. His prominence comes from making the path to success look achievable, even when the stakes are high.

## Huda Kattan: From Beauty Blogger to Billion-Dollar Brand

Huda Kattan took her passion for beauty and turned it into a billion-dollar empire. Originally a makeup artist and beauty blogger, Huda started by sharing makeup tutorials and reviews, quickly amassing a loyal fanbase. Recognizing the demand, she launched her own beauty line, Huda Beauty, which has since become one of the top beauty brands worldwide. What makes Huda's story remarkable is her approach to sharing her journey—the ups, the downs, and her insights into running a global business. Through her social media, Huda doesn't just sell makeup; she shares her entrepreneurial journey, inspiring fans to believe in their own potential. For Huda, wealth is about creating something people genuinely love and feel a part of, and her transparency has made her one of the most relatable yet aspirational influencers in the beauty world.

These influencers have done more than just accumulate followers; they've crafted entire lifestyles and narratives that people around the world want to be a part of. They've redefined the concept of wealth by curating an experience, a story, and a connection that feels both exclusive and accessible, all at the same time.

As we see, wealth, in the 21st century, is increasingly fluid. It's no longer just a fixed position or status; it's about maintaining the perception of success. Lifestyle influencer, Emma Chamberlain might have started with simple, no-frills YouTube vlogs, but she's turned herself into a full-blown lifestyle brand. Emma's charm lies in how "real" she feels. She shows up on camera without a script, edits her own videos, and has a quirky, relatable style that feels refreshingly genuine. But as she's evolved, so has her image. Now, you'll find Emma on magazine covers, partnering with Louis Vuitton, and serving as a style icon for Gen Z. Her success is in the balance—she's glamorous but still approachable, making high-end fashion and luxury experiences seem within reach for everyday people.

However, this obsession with visibility also raises questions. Is the financial glamour we see today genuine, or is it a carefully curated illusion? The answer, of course, is that it's both. Wealth, in this new era, is increasingly about the stories we tell, the narratives we create, and the images we project. In the world of social media, it's not enough to simply have wealth—you have to show it, market it, and sell it as part of a larger story about who you are and what you stand for.

## The New Wealth Icons: Entrepreneurs, Influencers, and Social Media Moguls

In the 21st century, wealth is no longer simply inherited; it is self-made. Entrepreneurs have become the new titans of industry, rising from humble beginnings to become some of the wealthiest and most influential individuals in the world. Unlike the industrial magnates of the 19th century, whose wealth was often built on raw materials, manufacturing, or natural resources, today's billionaires are largely driven by innovation, technology, and ideas. They are not just business owners; they are cultural icons whose every move is watched, analyzed, and copied.

At the forefront of this new generation of wealth creators are figures like Elon Musk, Jeff Bezos, Mark Zuckerberg, and Jack Dorsey—the faces of Silicon Valley and the digital revolution. These individuals have become symbols of the American Dream, embodying the idea that anyone, regardless of background, can achieve extraordinary success through ingenuity and hard work. But their rise to power is not just about what they've accomplished in the tech world—it's also about how they've harnessed the power of personal branding to build their fortunes.

Musk, for example, has turned his ventures like Tesla and SpaceX into much more than just companies; they are parts of his identity. Musk is as famous for his bold statements on Twitter and his public persona as he is for his companies' innovations. In many ways, he represents the new model of wealth in the 21st century—one that is intertwined with media, influence, and the ability to shape public opinion.

Similarly, Jeff Bezos redefined the way we think about business success through Amazon, but his story doesn't end with the company. He's also become a media mogul, with the purchase of The Washington Post, as well as a symbol of the billionaire class. His journey to becoming the wealthiest person on Earth is as much about his rise to prominence in the public eye as it is about Amazon's growth.

But it's not just entrepreneurs who are reshaping the idea of wealth in America today. The explosion of social media has given rise to a new class of wealth icons—those who have gained financial success and recognition through online platforms. Figures like Chiara Ferragni, and Dan Bilzerian have built empires on social media, turning their personal brands into highly profitable businesses. For them, wealth is no longer just about the products they sell; it's about their social influence, the lifestyle they curate, and the image they project to their followers.

The ability to create wealth through visibility and influence is a key feature of the Gilded Revival. As we'll explore in the chapters to come, the wealth creators of the 21st century are no longer just entrepreneurs—they are also media moguls, content creators, and influencers who understand that wealth is about more than just money; it's about cultivating the right image and shaping how the world perceives success.

## A Shift in Values: The Return of Financial Aspiration

But what drives this resurgence of financial glamour? It's more than just technology, entrepreneurship, and social media. It's a shift in cultural values. The 2020s mark a period where Americans, especially millennials and Gen Z, are increasingly valuing wealth as an attainable goal rather than something to be ashamed of. This era represents a new type of American Dream, one where financial success is not seen as a byproduct of privilege but as something that can be earned through hard work, creativity, and perseverance.

The shift towards financial openness, luxury, and public wealth is not just about the wealthy showing off; it's about aspiration. In today's world, wealth is not only something to be earned—it's something to be desired. With access to endless streams of content, social media influencers, and business moguls, today's generation is more driven than ever to build their own versions of wealth, inspired by the icons of the digital age. Whether it's the pursuit of the self-made fortune or the craving for a luxury lifestyle, today's world is one where financial glamour is no longer hidden behind closed doors but is celebrated on the world stage.

In the next chapters, we will explore how the Gilded Revival is not just a rebirth of the past but also a new era of wealth—one that celebrates the individual, embraces visibility, and offers new models of success that are more inclusive, more digitally savvy, and more aspirational than ever before.

## Chapter 3.1: The New Age of Real Estate: Reimagining the Luxury Home

### The Shift from "Home" to "Lifestyle Asset"

When we think of luxury real estate, the first images that often come to mind are grand mansions, sprawling estates, and breathtaking penthouses with views of the skyline. These homes, built with impeccable craftsmanship and featuring opulent finishes, have long been symbols of wealth. Yet, the idea of luxury real estate has evolved significantly in recent years. What was once simply a place of residence, a symbol of financial success, has transformed into something much more powerful: a carefully curated lifestyle asset.

In today's world, luxury homes are not just about the materials—whether marble floors or gold-plated faucets—they are about the entire experience of living in them. Homes have become a direct reflection of the owner's identity, personality, and, often, social aspirations. In fact, many of today's luxury buyers view their homes as an extension of their personal brand, and as a result, the concept of what constitutes a "luxury home" is increasingly tied to the lifestyle it provides rather than just the price tag.

The shift from home as a "living space" to a "lifestyle asset" represents a profound change in how people perceive the concept of homeownership. Historically, a house was simply a place to live—an investment, perhaps, but primarily functional. In the modern age, luxury real estate has become a way to express identity. It is no longer just a place to reside, but an experience to be had. The luxury buyer is not just looking for a place to call home; they are seeking a lifestyle, a manifestation of their aspirations and personal values.

Consider the rise of branded residences, such as the Four Seasons Private Residences or the Aman Residences in Miami, New York, and Los Angeles. These developments go beyond providing four walls and a roof. They offer an immersive experience. The allure of living in a Four Seasons building, is not just about access to a fancy address or luxurious accommodations; it's about the brand's promise of unparalleled service, seamless comfort, and the ability to integrate one's daily life with a level of opulence typically reserved for the world's most exclusive hotels. For the buyer, the residence becomes a status symbol in itself—an artifact of a lifestyle that is woven into every aspect of their existence.

Take, for example, the One57 Penthouse in New York City, also known as the "Billionaire's Building." With panoramic views of Central Park, a private elevator, and interior designed by the renowned designer Thomas Juul-Hansen, it's more than just a home. It's a symbol of affluence and exclusivity, offering a living experience that few can even imagine. The location and design are spectacular, but it's the lifestyle that makes this residence a premium asset—from world-class concierge services to in-house amenities such as a spa, a yoga studio, and a fitness center that rival the most elite boutique hotels.

Luxury real estate has also adapted to the changing tastes of wealthy buyers, where "luxury" means something much deeper than just materials. Today's affluent buyers are increasingly prioritizing spaces that align with their personal values, which often means emphasizing design, sustainability, and connection to nature. The Greenwich Street Project in New York City, for example, includes sustainable design features including rainwater harvesting systems and energy-efficient systems. For today's wealthy buyer, a home is no longer just an asset—it's a lifestyle statement that reflects both financial capability and cultural sophistication.

## The Growth of "Experience-Driven" Real Estate

Luxury real estate has also shifted dramatically to embrace the concept of experience-driven living. The modern home is not only designed for comfort and aesthetics, but it also offers a fully immersive experience for its residents, akin to staying at a luxury hotel or resort. Rooftop gardens, private spas, curated art collections, exclusive lounges, and even private cinemas are now the norm in many luxury developments.

Where once the focus was on traditional luxury features like marble floors and intricate woodwork, today's elite consumers are more interested in the experiences they can enjoy within the confines of their homes. These spaces are increasingly designed to mirror the offerings of a high-end resort or boutique hotel—offering everything one might need within their own residence.

For instance, one of the most spectacular examples of experience-driven real estate is The Park Grove Residences in Miami. These properties feature private gardens, curated artwork, and high-end luxury amenities including a Michelin-starred restaurant on-site, wellness spaces, and an infinity-edge pool overlooking Biscayne Bay. The goal here is not simply to offer a living space; it's to offer an entire lifestyle experience, one that integrates luxury, leisure, and wellness all under one roof. The Aman Residences in Miami, located in the heart of Brickell, take this concept even further, providing owners with exclusive access to the Aman spa and wellness center, as well as private chef services and bespoke concierge arrangements.

Real estate developers have come to understand that today's high-net-worth individuals no longer want to simply own a property—they want access to experiences that match the lifestyle they've worked hard to achieve. The luxury home is now seen as a venue for daily living that offers a curated set of experiences that elevate one's lifestyle. Amenities including private yoga studios, wine cellars, and gourmet kitchens are becoming standard. And beyond these, some properties have raised the bar to include features such as in-house spa treatments, art exhibits curated by world-renowned curators, or even members-only clubs with unparalleled access to exclusive events and experiences.

Additionally, the Alila Villas Uluwatu in Bali, Indonesia, offers private villas with fully integrated wellness programs, including fitness activities, nutrition consultations, and stress-relieving therapies, aimed at making a stay both luxurious and restorative. While not technically a "residential" home, it offers a glimpse into how developments are moving toward blending leisure, relaxation, and convenience with exclusive real estate offerings.

Luxury buyers are now looking for homes that embody both style and substance, not only offering the height of luxury living, but offering that luxury in a way that enhances their daily lives in profound ways. From curated spaces that reflect personal aesthetics to wellness amenities that integrate health and leisure, today's luxury home is less about a building and more about an experience.

## Smart Homes and Technology Integration

In today's luxury real estate market, the concept of a smart home is no longer a futuristic luxury—it's an essential part of high-end living. Technology is now seamlessly integrated into homes to create a convenient, secure, and customizable experience for the homeowner. Buyers are seeking homes where technology works behind the scenes, enhancing their lifestyle without drawing attention away from the aesthetics or design.

At the forefront of this transformation is the integration of automated systems for lighting, security, entertainment, and climate control. The smart home is no longer just about having voice-activated lighting or smart thermostats—it's about creating a fully automated, tailored experience for homeowners. In some cases, technology is used to make everyday life more convenient, such as remote-controlled window blinds, automated coffee machines, or homes that can be pre-warmed or pre-cooled through a mobile app before the owner even steps foot inside.

The Samsung Smart Home systems are leading the way in this area, offering homebuyers the ability to automate nearly every aspect of their homes, from security to entertainment. These systems are often integrated into high-end luxury residences, where advanced smart home automation has become a defining feature of the overall luxury experience. Homes equipped with AI-powered systems can anticipate the owner's needs, adjusting lighting, temperature, and entertainment systems based on preferences, all through voice commands or a simple touch of a button.

In many ultra-luxury homes, technology goes beyond just automation—it's about personalization. The Ritz-Carlton Residences in Los Angeles have been integrated with high-tech home systems that allow residents to customize lighting, adjust room temperatures, and even control sound systems remotely. The smart kitchen technology allows owners to control appliances via an app, making their culinary experiences smoother and more convenient.

Moreover, technology has become a status symbol in its own right. Homes equipped with state-of-the-art sound systems, home theaters, and high-end surveillance systems not only provide security and comfort but also emphasize the homeowner's connection to the latest and most advanced technology. The Miele brand, known for its luxury kitchen appliances, is increasingly in demand among high-end buyers, with its sophisticated designs offering both high performance and advanced connectivity.

In some of the most exclusive residences, homes are also designed to be energy-efficient through technology that reduces environmental impact. In the case of The Greenwich Village Residences, eco-friendly systems such as solar panels, rainwater collection systems, and energy-efficient HVAC units are seamlessly integrated into the design, allowing the homeowner to enjoy both luxury and sustainability. This commitment to eco-conscious living appeals to a new generation of luxury buyers who demand both style and sustainability.

## Concluding thoughts

The luxury real estate market has undergone a dramatic transformation in recent years, shifting from a traditional focus on bricks and mortar to one that emphasizes experience, lifestyle, and innovation. Today's luxury homes are not just places to live—they are experiential assets that provide the modern wealthy with a complete lifestyle. As buyers increasingly demand more from their homes—whether in the form of smart technology, wellness features, or high-end amenities—luxury real estate has become an evolving market that mirrors the changing desires and aspirations of the affluent.

## Chapter 3.2: The Evolution of High-End Fashion and Personal Style

High-end fashion has long been a marker of wealth, taste, and status, but in recent years, it has undergone a dramatic transformation. Fashion is no longer just about wearing the latest trends; it has evolved into a sophisticated investment vehicle, with luxury items often appreciating in value over time. At the same time, the conversation around sustainability has reshaped the notion of luxury, introducing new expectations for ethics, environmental impact, and transparency.

Fashion influencer Doina Ciobanu highlights the evolving definition of luxury in the fashion industry, stating, "Luxury is no longer just about exclusivity and price; it's about knowing the origins of your clothing, the materials used, and the craftsmanship involved." This perspective underscores the growing consumer demand for ethical practices, environmental responsibility, and transparency in luxury fashion.

## Luxury Fashion as an Investment

Traditionally, high-end fashion was seen as the epitome of status—brands including Chanel, Louis Vuitton, and Hermès symbolized affluence and exclusivity. The notion was simple: the more expensive the item, the more luxurious it was. Over time, however, luxury fashion has evolved into something much more sophisticated: an investment. Today, luxury brands are creating items that not only make a statement in terms of style, but also appreciate in value over time. This shift has transformed luxury fashion into a true financial asset, with collectors viewing limited-edition pieces, high-end handbags, and iconic watches as investments that can yield substantial returns.

One of the clearest examples of this phenomenon is the market for luxury handbags. The brand Hermès has long been associated with exclusivity, but in recent years, their products have become sought-after financial assets. The Hermès Birkin bag, which once served as a simple luxury accessory, has become one of the most famous investment items in the fashion world. Over the last two decades, the value of a Birkin bag has far outpaced the stock market, with certain bags appreciating in value by over 500%. For example, in 2020, a rare Birkin Himalaya (crafted from crocodile leather and featuring platinum hardware) was sold at auction for $380,000—a price that many consider to be an investment, rather than simply a purchase.

Similarly, the Rolex Submariner watch, an iconic symbol of wealth and status, has seen consistent appreciation over the years. What was once simply a high-end timepiece is now considered an investment object. The Rolex Daytona, is often sold at auction for multiples of its original retail price, with certain models, such as the Paul Newman Daytona, fetching upwards of $17 million. This transformation of watches and handbags into appreciating assets has reshaped the way high-end fashion is perceived, blurring the lines between personal style and financial strategy.

Another area where luxury fashion has gained traction as an investment is the limited edition and one-of-a-kind market. Brands including Louis Vuitton and Gucci regularly release limited-edition pieces, often in collaboration with renowned artists or designers. Louis Vuitton's collaboration with Jeff Koons, produced a line of bags featuring reproductions of famous artworks, and the bags quickly became highly sought after. The bags, though expensive at the time of release, are now fetching premium prices on resale platforms, with some items increasing in value by as much as 200%.

These collaborations are part of a larger trend in which luxury fashion houses are increasingly producing items that are designed to be collector's pieces. High-end streetwear brands like Supreme and Off-White are contributing to this shift, releasing highly limited-run items that create a sense of urgency and exclusivity, driving up the resale market for these pieces. As a result, items that once might have been considered niche fashion or trend-driven are now seen as valuable commodities.

The rise of the secondary market, especially platforms StockX, The RealReal, and Vestiaire Collective, has further fueled this phenomenon. These platforms allow consumers to buy and sell pre-owned luxury goods, further cementing luxury fashion's role as an investment. According to StockX, the resale market for sneakers alone was worth over $2 billion in 2020, a figure that speaks to the increasing intersection of fashion and financial investment.

## Sustainable and Ethical Luxury

As wealth and financial power have become central to the world of luxury fashion, there has also been a growing emphasis on ethics and sustainability. The luxury industry, traditionally associated with exclusivity and environmental opulence, has increasingly found itself under scrutiny due to the harmful environmental impact of fashion production. From the exploitation of leather and silk, to the massive carbon footprint created by fast fashion, the fashion industry has been criticized for its unsustainable practices.

In response to these concerns, many high-end brands have started to embrace sustainable luxury, offering environmentally conscious products without sacrificing the premium quality that luxury consumers expect. This new wave of sustainability is not about sacrificing luxury—it's about creating luxury with integrity, where environmental impact is mitigated through responsible sourcing, ethical labor practices, and sustainable design.

One brand at the forefront of this movement is Stella McCartney, whose commitment to sustainable practices has been widely recognized. McCartney, a lifelong environmental advocate, has made sustainability a cornerstone of her brand. In 2019, McCartney released a collection made entirely from recycled materials. This collection, which included clothing, handbags, and accessories, used recycled polyester, organic cotton, and vegan leather. McCartney has also led efforts to eliminate fur from her designs, pushing the luxury industry toward cruelty-free fashion.

Similarly, Gucci has taken significant strides toward ethical production. In 2018, the brand announced its commitment to becoming more sustainable by pledging to reduce its environmental footprint. Gucci's commitment to transparency has included publishing an Environmental Profit and Loss (EP&L) report, detailing the impact of its operations on water usage, carbon emissions, and other environmental factors. Gucci also launched the Gucci Equilibrium platform, which showcases the brand's sustainability efforts, from responsible sourcing of materials to initiatives for reducing waste.

But it's not just large, established brands that are embracing sustainability; younger, smaller labels have also entered the luxury market with an emphasis on ethical production. Reformation, a brand known for its eco-friendly approach to fashion, produces its garments using organic cotton and recycled fabrics. The company is transparent about its supply chain, even showing consumers where and how each item is made. This emphasis on ethical production has helped Reformation build a loyal following, particularly among Millennials and Gen Z consumers, who are increasingly demanding accountability from the brands they support.

Another company leading the charge is Patagonia. Although more associated with outdoor wear, it is recognized for its commitment to sustainability and ethical practices in the fashion world. Patagonia has pioneered the use of recycled materials in its clothing, including jackets made from recycled plastic bottles, and has a Worn Wear program, encouraging customers to buy used Patagonia products and trade in their old gear for new ones. Patagonia has also committed to fair labor practices, ensuring that workers in its supply chain receive fair wages and work in safe conditions.

The move toward sustainable luxury is not just about eco-friendly production; it also involves an increasing awareness of circular fashion, which aims to keep clothing in circulation longer through repurposing and recycling. The luxury resale market, mentioned earlier, is a key component of this movement. Vintage stores including What Goes Around Comes Around and Café de Flore in Paris, sell pre-owned designer goods, which allows for the reuse and recycling of items that might otherwise end up in landfills.

In addition to the growing demand for sustainable products, consumers are also pushing for ethical labor practices. Today's affluent shoppers are increasingly aware of the working conditions under which their clothing is produced, and they are more likely to support brands that prioritize fair wages, safe working conditions, and respect for workers' rights.

## The Influence of Streetwear and High Fashion

In the world of fashion, the rise of streetwear has disrupted the traditional hierarchy of luxury. What was once considered an underground, rebellious fashion movement—rooted in skateboard culture, hip-hop, and urban street style—has now become a dominant force in high-end fashion. Over the past decade, streetwear has infiltrated the luxury market in ways that have fundamentally altered the very definition of what it means to be "luxurious."

A key moment in this shift came with the partnership between Gucci and Supreme. In 2018, these two brands—one known for its high-fashion heritage, and the other for its street-savvy, youth-focused appeal—came together to create a limited-edition collection that sold out in a matter of minutes. The collaboration marked a melding of cultures, where luxury and street culture were no longer opposing forces but were intertwined, attracting a new generation of buyers that valued exclusivity and urban street style.

Another high-profile example is the partnership between Nike and Off-White, the fashion label created by Virgil Abloh, which became the epitome of luxury streetwear. Abloh, who was named artistic director of Louis Vuitton's men's wear in 2018, has blurred the lines between streetwear and high fashion, designing sneakers, handbags, and apparel that combine the two worlds. The Off-White x Nike Air Presto, a collaboration between Abloh's brand and Nike, became one of the most coveted items in the fashion world, with limited-edition sneakers fetching thousands of dollars on resale platforms.

These collaborations have not only democratized high fashion but have also made it accessible to younger consumers who might not have traditionally been able to afford the high-end couture pieces once associated with wealth and exclusivity. As streetwear continues to merge with luxury fashion, affluent millennials and Gen Z consumers are increasingly seeking fashion that blends opulence with authenticity, creating a new paradigm where high-end fashion is not just about clothes, but about self-expression and cultural relevance.

## Concluding thoughts

The evolution of high-end fashion and personal style is a testament to the changing nature of luxury itself. Fashion has become multi-faceted—a blend of investment, sustainability, and self-expression. What was once purely about exclusive designer labels and status symbols has now expanded into a dynamic world where luxury is about more than just what you wear—it's about how it reflects your values, your ambitions, and your personal narrative. As streetwear influences high fashion, and as the demand for sustainable luxury continues to grow, the future of fashion will undoubtedly be marked by crossover collaborations, new definitions of luxury, and sophisticated consumerism that embrace both individualism and the collective need for a more responsible, equitable future.

## Chapter 3.3: Luxury Travel: Experiences Over Possessions

In the last few decades, the definition of luxury has evolved in profound ways. Once synonymous with opulent possessions—immaculate mansions, diamond-studded jewelry, designer wardrobes—luxury now often extends beyond material goods to something more intangible: experiences. As the world has shifted, particularly in the post-millennial era, affluent individuals are no longer primarily seeking to accumulate wealth through items; they are increasingly investing in unique, high-end travel experiences that cater to their desires for exclusivity, adventure, and personal connection to the world. The burgeoning luxury travel industry reflects this dramatic shift, where personalized, one-of-a-kind experiences are prized over mere possessions. From private islands to space tourism, from eco-resorts to bespoke safaris, travelers now seek experiences that are as exceptional as they are transformative.

This chapter explores the rise of the ultra-luxury travel sector, focusing on the demand for experiential travel and the personalization that characterizes it. In addition to this, we will explore how luxury travelers are increasingly seeking destinations and experiences that are not only rare and luxurious but also contribute to environmental conservation and sustainability. Travel is becoming a way to express one's status, values, and unique desires, with an emphasis on creating moments that transcend traditional notions of luxury.

## The Rise of "Ultra-Luxury" Experiences

The luxury travel market has undergone a dramatic shift over the past several decades. Once a sector defined by extravagant five-star hotels, gourmet dining, and spa experiences, today's ultra-luxury travel is about offering experiences that transcend the ordinary and provide access to places, adventures, and moments that few others can ever imagine. These unique and often bespoke experiences are not just about indulgence but about exclusivity, personal transformation, and the desire to explore the world in a way that is both exceptional and intimate.

Private Island Rentals have become one of the quintessential offerings in ultra-luxury travel. This is not simply about booking an extravagant vacation home but about enjoying a fully secluded, personalized experience in a completely private and exclusive environment. Necker Island, owned by billionaire Richard Branson, offers visitors a chance to rent the entire island in the British Virgin Islands for a private retreat, with prices starting at $75,000 per night. The island provides not only luxurious accommodations but also a full range of curated experiences, from private yacht charters and water sports to intimate dinners with world-class chefs. As wealthy individuals increasingly seek privacy and personal space, Necker Island represents a model for the future of ultra-luxury: solitude combined with opulence.

Similarly, in the Maldives, several private islands cater exclusively to high-net-worth individuals. Properties such as Velaa Private Island offer world-class amenities, including overwater villas with private pools, personalized butlers, and even submarine experiences. It is not just about relaxation but about unforgettable adventures in a pristine, highly exclusive environment. Velaa offers guests the chance to enjoy ultra-luxury combined with adventures such as deep-sea diving, underwater wine cellars, and private yoga classes.

Exclusive safaris also represent a prime example of luxury travel experiences that go far beyond simple leisure. In Africa, high-net-worth individuals can experience safaris in the most remote and pristine regions, ensuring their exposure to the natural world remains untouched by other tourists. Singita Grumeti, located in Tanzania's Serengeti National Park, is one such destination where guests can have access to private game drives, accompanied by expert guides, in vehicles designed for maximum comfort and unobtrusiveness. Guests can also enjoy private hot air balloon rides over the Serengeti, where they witness the Great Migration from an intimate perspective. This experience is about much more than luxury; it is about connection to nature in its purest form.

The concept of space tourism has added an entirely new dimension to ultra-luxury travel. In recent years, Blue Origin, Virgin Galactic, and SpaceX have transformed the impossible into reality, offering wealthy individuals the chance to leave Earth and venture into space. A Virgin Galactic flight, for instance, offers a brief journey to space with a price tag of approximately $450,000 per seat. The experience includes several days of training and preparation, culminating in a suborbital flight that provides a few minutes of weightlessness. For the affluent, this is not just about adventure—it's about being part of an exclusive club that pushes the boundaries of what is possible, offering an entirely new type of bragging right.

The market for these ultra-luxury experiences is growing rapidly, driven by a new class of wealthy individuals who are no longer content with simply visiting famous landmarks but are seeking more intimate, immersive, and once-in-a-lifetime experiences that are carefully curated to fit their personal desires.

## Sustainable and Experiential Travel

While the desire for exclusive and exceptional experiences continues to shape the ultra-luxury travel industry, there is a growing demand for experiences that also take into account environmental sustainability and social responsibility. High-end consumers, especially those belonging to younger generations like Millennials and Gen Z, are increasingly conscious of the environmental impact of their travel. Today's wealthy traveler is less likely to prioritize material goods and more inclined to align their travel choices with values of sustainability and conservation.

In response to this, a new wave of eco-luxury resorts has emerged that offer exceptional experiences while also prioritizing environmental conservation. One such example is Soneva Fushi, an eco-resort in the Maldives that combines luxury with sustainable practices. Soneva Fushi has developed a strong reputation for offering private villas built using sustainable materials, solar power, and water conservation technologies. The resort has also launched its own "Soneva Foundation", which supports environmental projects and promotes ocean conservation. Guests at Soneva Fushi can enjoy the luxury of private beach resorts while also engaging in eco-friendly practices like snorkeling with marine biologists and participating in beach clean-up projects. This type of experience blends luxury with social responsibility, offering travelers a way to enjoy the very best of nature while ensuring that nature itself is protected.

The Brando in French Polynesia is another example of an ultra-luxury, sustainable destination. Located on the private island of Tetiaroa, this resort was built with a strong emphasis on sustainability. The island's energy needs are met entirely by solar panels and coconut oil biofuel, and local, organic food is sourced from the island's farm. The Brando offers a fully private, exclusive retreat, where guests can explore the island's lush environment while engaging with conservation initiatives. A key element of this resort is its commitment to protecting the surrounding coral reefs, making it an ideal destination for those looking for an eco-luxury experience that supports both personal well-being and planetary health.

Beyond resort-focused experiences, the demand for eco-conscious travel extends to entire destinations. Costa Rica, for example, has become a mecca for luxury travelers looking to explore natural beauty while also contributing to conservation efforts. The country is home to some of the most biodiverse rainforests, and travelers can enjoy high-end eco-lodges like Lapa Rios and El Silencio Lodge, both of which offer extraordinary experiences like rainforest treks, wildlife viewing, and private waterfalls, all while maintaining strong environmental standards. Many luxury travel companies now offer green itineraries where guests can engage in conservation efforts such as sea turtle conservation projects or carbon offset programs.

## The Personalization of Luxury Travel

In today's luxury travel market, it's not just about where you go, but how the experience is tailored to your specific desires. Personalization has become the defining characteristic of high-end travel, with travelers now seeking experiences that are as unique and individualized as they are. Gone are the days of generic hotel stays and pre-planned itineraries. Now, the affluent demand that every detail of their trip, from flight preferences to meal choices, is meticulously curated to suit their preferences.

"People want things that are curated to them," says Julia Carter, founder of the luxury travel agency Craft Travel. "They don't want cookie-cutter experiences; they don't want to go somewhere where everything feels like it could be AI-generated."

Abercrombie & Kent, a leader in the luxury travel space, is known for offering highly personalized itineraries that cater to every possible whim of their clients. Whether it's arranging a private concert at the Colosseum in Rome or organizing a tailored wine-tasting tour in Bordeaux, Abercrombie & Kent's specialists design travel experiences that are completely bespoke. The company's Private Jet Journeys program offers customers the opportunity to fly in luxury aboard a fully equipped private jet while experiencing personalized tours in destinations around the globe. These experiences include private art showings, behind-the-scenes access to cultural events, and bespoke culinary experiences with top chefs. No request is too small or too extravagant, making it a prime example of how luxury travel is becoming personalized to an extreme degree.

Similarly, companies like Black Tomato specialize in offering hyper-personalized travel experiences for high-net-worth clients. Black Tomato's "Get Lost" program offers adventurous travelers the chance to create their own private hideaways in remote destinations. The company curates every aspect of the journey, from private flights to personalized itineraries, ensuring that travelers receive a truly bespoke adventure. Whether it's a stay in a luxury tent in Antarctica or a remote helicopter trip to a private Swiss chalet, Black Tomato focuses on curating adventures that are aligned with the individual's passions, ensuring that the experience feels deeply personal and exclusive.

The key to personalization is not just the luxury of choice but the promise of customization that speaks to the client's values and lifestyle. Whether it's food preferences, health and wellness needs, or cultural sensitivities, the luxury travel sector is increasingly catering to travelers who expect every facet of their journey to be tailored specifically to them. Concierge services and travel advisors are now more adept at creating experiential itineraries that fit the interests and aspirations of their clients.

## Concluding thoughts

The luxury travel industry has undergone a radical transformation, with a renewed focus on offering experiences that are both exclusive and personalized. Whether it's lounging on a private island, embarking on a once-in-a-lifetime safari, or exploring the edges of space, ultra-luxury travelers are seeking access to adventures that go beyond the material world and offer rare, meaningful moments. As luxury travelers continue to seek out experiences that are unique, personal, and sustainable, the very nature of what it means to be "wealthy" has evolved. Today's affluent individual is not simply defined by the goods they own but by the rare, unforgettable experiences they are able to create and enjoy. This shift in focus from possessions to experiences marks the next evolution in the pursuit of luxury—an evolution that blends exclusivity, personalization, and responsibility, ultimately changing how we think about wealth in the 21st century.

# Chapter 3.4: Fine Dining and the Art of Exclusive Culinary Experiences

In the world of luxury, there is perhaps no better example of refinement, status, and sophistication than fine dining. However, in recent years, the notion of what constitutes a luxury dining experience has undergone a dramatic shift. The luxury consumer, particularly in the 21st century, seeks more than just exquisite meals prepared by renowned chefs in Michelin-starred restaurants. Today's affluent diners are looking for multi-sensory culinary adventures, experiences that push the boundaries of taste, presentation, and personalization. As food culture evolves, high-end dining has shifted from being an exclusive meal to an immersive experience, one that incorporates not just taste, but sight, sound, and smell, transforming an evening at a restaurant into an unforgettable journey.

In this chapter, we explore the evolution of luxury dining, examining the rise of culinary adventures, the growing trend of private chefs and curated dining events, and the increasing focus on sustainability and local sourcing in high-end cuisine. Through specific examples, we will explore how modern luxury dining is not only about the food itself but the experience—the exclusive moments, personalized touches, and the atmosphere that transforms a meal into an event of significance.

## The Shift from Fine Dining to Culinary Adventure

In the past, luxury dining was primarily associated with gourmet food prepared in exclusive settings, with established rules of haute cuisine governing the atmosphere and experience. Michelin stars, haute couture menus, and classic French techniques defined the pinnacle of fine dining. However, the expectations of the modern wealthy consumer have evolved. Today's luxury food enthusiast is not only seeking an exceptional meal but an experience—an event that engages all the senses and provides lasting memories.

One of the key movements in this evolution has been the shift toward tasting menus and multi-sensory dining experiences. Chefs are now incorporating elements like interactive dining, sight-specific design, and soundscapes into their menus. The result is a transformation from a traditional meal to an immersive culinary adventure, where the diner becomes part of the experience rather than a passive consumer.

Take, for example, The Fat Duck in Bray, England, led by chef Heston Blumenthal. Known for its avant-garde culinary approach, the restaurant offers a multi-course tasting menu that is more about playful exploration than simply food. Guests are treated to dishes like "Sound of the Sea", where diners listen to the sounds of the ocean through earphones while tasting a dish that mimics the flavors of the sea, including seaweed and shellfish. The experience is as much about sensory engagement as it is about taste, inviting diners to engage with the food in a way that is both intellectual and emotional. This approach to dining is immersive, and it elevates the act of eating from a necessity to an art form.

Similarly, El Celler de Can Roca in Girona, Spain, led by the Roca brothers, has become a global symbol of innovative luxury dining. While the restaurant is renowned for its exceptional Catalan cuisine, it also emphasizes a sense of storytelling in its presentations. The meal is not merely about eating; it's about taking a journey through flavors, memories, and textures, with each course evoking a story. In one memorable dish, the restaurant serves a liquid olive, a spherical olive that bursts in the mouth, representing the perfect balance between innovation and tradition. This shift from dining to experiential gastronomy is a hallmark of modern luxury, where patrons are not just tasting food—they are living it.

Another fascinating example of experiential dining can be found at Narisawa in Tokyo, Japan. Chef Yoshihiro Narisawa is known for his "Innovative Satoyama Cuisine," which combines local, seasonal ingredients with sustainable farming practices. The dining experience at Narisawa isn't just a meal; it's an exploration of the natural world and the changing seasons. The menu changes constantly, reflecting the very essence of nature—an evolving, multi-layered sensory experience that connects the diner to both the earth and the seasons. For instance, diners may experience a dish that is designed to mimic the transition from spring to summer, showcasing local ingredients like fresh herbs, wild mushrooms, and spring vegetables. Each dish tells a story about the land, the seasons, and the connection between food and nature.

The appeal of these multi-sensory dining experiences is clear: affluent diners are seeking food that stimulates the mind, engages the senses, and offers a deeper connection to the meal and the environment around it. Fine dining is no longer just about the food on the plate but about the total experience—the taste, the textures, the sounds, the visuals, and the atmosphere that come together to create something memorable.

## Rise of Private Chefs and Curated Events

As the desire for exclusive experiences has grown, so has the demand for private dining. The private chef trend has surged in popularity, particularly among high-net-worth individuals who value both exclusivity and personalization. Hiring a private chef allows clients to bypass traditional fine dining establishments and enjoy bespoke, curated meals tailored to their preferences, dietary requirements, and the unique atmosphere they wish to create.

Private chefs are hired for a variety of events—intimate dinner parties, private yacht gatherings, destination events, and even for extended stays at luxury residences. The concept of curated events has become an increasingly popular way to celebrate milestones, entertain friends, or simply enjoy a luxurious evening without the public gaze.

One example of a successful private dining experience is Chef's Table by Juan Carlos Reyes, a private dining experience hosted in the luxurious homes of affluent clients around the world. Chef Reyes has catered to celebrities, business moguls, and royalty, offering a dining experience that is completely tailored to the host's preferences. Each event is an immersive experience where the menu is based on personal tastes and dietary restrictions, with every detail considered, from the wines paired with each course to the decor and ambiance of the room.

Similarly, private chefs can now be hired for luxury yacht charters, where the entire dining experience is curated based on the destination and the client's preferences. Companies like Chef's Table at Sea offer the opportunity to have a world-class chef on board, preparing custom menus using fresh, local ingredients that reflect the culture of the places visited. This shift to private, curated dining allows for an even greater level of personalization and intimacy—qualities that traditional fine dining cannot always deliver.

Beyond the home or yacht, the destination dining experience has also grown in popularity. For example, some luxury resorts offer the chance to have meals prepared on-site by personal chefs, who design special menus based on local ingredients, custom flavors, and the guest's desires. In the Maldives, resorts like One&Only Reethi Rah offer private beach dinners, where a chef will prepare an evening gourmet meal right on the sand, lit by lanterns, making the meal an experience that goes beyond food to encompass atmosphere and location. Here, guests are not only tasting exquisite food but are part of a carefully constructed event that engages multiple senses—further enhancing the personalized experience.

## Sustainability and Local Sourcing in High-End Cuisine

As the luxury dining scene becomes more focused on personalized experiences, there is a growing demand for sustainable and locally sourced ingredients. Today's high-end diners are not just concerned with the taste of the food—they want to know where it comes from, how it's produced, and whether it aligns with their values. The intersection of luxury dining and sustainability has led to a new era of conscious cuisine, where the emphasis is on authenticity, seasonality, and a deep connection to place.

One example of this is Blue Hill at Stone Barns, a restaurant located in Pocantico Hills, New York. Under the direction of chef Dan Barber, Blue Hill has become a pioneer in the farm-to-table movement and a leader in sustainable dining. The restaurant sources much of its produce from the adjacent Stone Barns Center for Food and Agriculture, ensuring that everything served is locally grown, seasonally appropriate, and produced in an environmentally conscious way. Barber's approach to dining emphasizes connection to the land and a respect for seasonality, teaching diners that true luxury in food is not just about extravagance but about being attuned to the natural rhythms of the earth. Guests can enjoy dishes made with ingredients harvested that very morning, giving them a direct and authentic connection to the food they eat.

In Denmark, Noma, led by Rene Redzepi, is another restaurant that has redefined luxury dining by focusing heavily on local sourcing and sustainability. Noma's menu is deeply tied to the seasons and is known for featuring ingredients that are foraged from the wild—whether it's herbs from the woods or seaweed from the coastline. By incorporating fermentation techniques, Noma also brings out new flavors from local, often overlooked, ingredients. This emphasis on hyper-locality is not just a trend but a way to create food that is uniquely tied to its environment, making the dining experience deeply connected to both the place and the season.

Sustainability is now seen as a luxury in its own right, with high-end consumers increasingly valuing the integrity of their food's source. Sustainable menus, eco-conscious packaging, and a focus on reducing food waste are becoming key pillars of modern fine dining. As a result, some of the world's most renowned chefs are shifting their approach to focus on creating food that is not only exquisite but also responsible and reflective of the values and consciousness of the modern wealthy consumer.

## Concluding thoughts

The world of fine dining has undergone a transformation, with luxury dining now becoming an immersive, personalized, and multi-sensory experience that goes beyond food to include atmosphere, storytelling, and connection. From avant-garde tasting menus to private chef experiences, today's affluent diners seek experiential gastronomy that blends art, taste, and emotion. As the demand for sustainability and local sourcing rises, modern luxury dining embraces a future where food is not just about indulgence but about connection to nature, seasonality, and culture.

The evolution of luxury dining reflects a broader cultural shift—where wealth is increasingly tied not to the accumulation of material goods but to the pursuit of exclusive experiences and meaningful moments. As this trend continues to develop, the world of high-end cuisine will continue to redefine what it means to dine in luxury, offering unforgettable experiences that push the boundaries of taste, sensation, and personalization.

## Chapter 3.5: The Exclusive World of Art, Collectibles, and High-End Hobbies

In the world of high-end luxury, the pursuit of wealth and status often transcends traditional forms of material consumption and enters a realm where art, collectibles, and exclusive hobbies serve as the ultimate symbols of sophistication, identity, and success. These pursuits not only showcase personal taste but also act as markers of social standing and investment. From rare works of art to vintage wines, custom yachts, and the latest in tech-driven collectibles like NFTs, the ultra-wealthy today are embracing a diverse array of passions that speak to their taste, their wealth, and their desire to participate in an exclusive, elite world.

As much as high-end fashion, luxury travel, and fine dining have redefined wealth aspiration, art collecting, luxury hobbies, and exclusive collectibles now occupy a place of prestige, offering both financial returns and cultural capital. This chapter delves into the evolving world of luxury art, high-end hobbies, and the emerging digital collectibles market. We will explore how art has become not just a form of cultural expression but a financial asset class and how niche hobbies, once considered the domain of the elite, have morphed into full-blown luxury pursuits. Lastly, we will look at how NFTs and digital art have revolutionized the concept of collectability, creating new avenues for wealth, status, and exclusivity in the 21st century.

## Art as a Status Symbol and Investment

For centuries, art has symbolized wealth, taste, and status. It has been the domain of royalty, noble families, and later, captains of industry, who amassed priceless collections to showcase their personal taste and power. But in recent years, art has evolved into a financial asset class, and it has been embraced by the ultra-wealthy not just for its cultural value but also for its ability to generate significant financial returns.

The world of art collecting today is an exclusive, highly competitive space, where wealthy individuals compete to acquire masterpieces and contemporary works that will not only enhance their social standing but also offer considerable returns as investments. Auction houses Christie's and Sotheby's have seen record-breaking sales, and iconic artists such as Jean-Michel Basquiat, Banksy, and David Hockney have entered the realm of high-end collectibles alongside more traditional names like Picasso and Van Gogh.

One of the most notable trends in modern art collecting is the focus on contemporary art, particularly pieces that reflect cultural relevance and have an investment potential. Take, for instance, Jean-Michel Basquiat, whose work has become a symbol of both artistic genius and financial success. In 2017, Basquiat's painting, "Untitled" (1982), sold for a record $110.5 million at auction, setting a new standard for contemporary art prices. This painting, like many of his works, has become more than just a piece of art—it is an investment vehicle, a cultural commodity, and a status symbol. For wealthy individuals, owning a Basquiat painting signals sophistication, cultural awareness, and an ability to navigate the world of high-end art.

Similarly, the works of Banksy, the elusive street artist, have risen to prominence as a symbol of both artistic rebellion and financial success.

Banksy's work challenges conventional ideas about art while achieving record-breaking sales at auction. One such sale occurred in 2018, when "Girl with a Balloon" was sold at Sotheby's for over £1 million. Just minutes after the gavel fell, the painting self-destructed as it was secretly rigged with a shredder hidden inside the frame. This stunt, however, only increased the painting's value, making it a true collector's item. For buyers, owning a Banksy is not just about having a piece of art—it's about being part of an exclusive club that appreciates cultural irony, rebellion, and high-value assets.

Art has thus become not only a vehicle for cultural expression but a highly lucrative investment. Wealthy collectors now view their art collections as part of their overall investment portfolio, much like real estate or stocks. Contemporary art has increasingly mirrored the world of alternative investments, where limited edition works and rare pieces become tangible assets whose value can appreciate substantially over time.

## The Rise of Niche Hobbies and High-End Gear

While art collecting remains a cornerstone of the luxury market, the concept of what constitutes a luxury hobby has expanded dramatically. The days when yachting, polo, and rare car collecting were the preserve of the super-rich have given way to a new era of luxury hobbies, where personal taste, exclusivity, and the thrill of ownership are key drivers. The emergence of high-end gear and specialized items for niche hobbies has been a defining trend in the wealth sector, with affluent individuals seeking to distinguish themselves by investing in exclusive experiences and premium products.

Take, for example, the world of yachting, which has long been associated with the ultimate status symbol. Today, the demand for luxury yachts has reached new heights, with brands like Feadship, Lürssen, and Oceanco creating some of the world's most coveted vessels. These yachts are not just about sailing; they are designed to be floating palaces, complete with spas, gyms, cinemas, and even helipads. The Azzam, a yacht built by Lürssen, holds the title of the world's largest private yacht at an astounding 180 meters (590 feet). It was built for an undisclosed member of the royal family of the UAE, and the vessel is valued at approximately $600 million. Yachting is no longer just a recreational activity; it has become an exclusive hobby for the ultra-wealthy, one that involves not just purchasing a yacht but cultivating a lifestyle of luxury cruising and oceanic adventures.

Similarly, the world of rare wine collecting has evolved from a niche hobby to a full-blown luxury pursuit. The demand for vintage wines has exploded, with wealthy collectors viewing wine not only as a refined pleasure but as an investment opportunity. The prices for rare wines, such as Romanée-Conti from Burgundy or Château Pétrus from Bordeaux, have surged in recent years. In fact, certain bottles have appreciated in value by over 1000% over the last two decades, making wine collecting a lucrative venture for the affluent. Auctions dedicated to fine wine, such as those held by Sotheby's and Bonhams, have become major events in the luxury market, attracting bidders from across the globe eager to acquire bottles that not only represent status but promise a significant return on investment.

The world of custom car racing and vintage car collecting also exemplifies the growing connection between luxury and hobbies. High-end automobiles, once seen as simply modes of transportation, have now evolved into highly sought-after collectibles, often commanding millions at auction. Ferraris, Porsches, and Lamborghinis have long been symbols of status, but their significance has grown with the rise of classic car auctions. For example, a 1955 Mercedes-Benz 300 SLR Uhlenhaut Coupe was sold for a record $143 million in May 2022, breaking records and setting new benchmarks in the world of luxury car collecting. The rarest of vintage cars now rival art and jewelry as investment vehicles, and the world of exclusive racing events like the Monaco Grand Prix has turned into a high-profile arena for wealthy hobbyists.

In many of these cases, these hobbies are not just about the passion for the activity itself but about curating a lifestyle of exclusivity. The gear and items associated with these pursuits are not just functional; they are markers of social status and wealth. Owning an elite yacht, vintage car, or rare wine bottle signals a connection to a world that is defined by luxury, taste, and financial power.

## NFTs and Digital Collectibles: The New Frontier of Luxury Collecting

As we venture deeper into the digital age, a new frontier of luxury collecting has emerged in the form of NFTs (Non-Fungible Tokens) and digital art. NFTs have taken the art world—and the luxury sector—by storm, opening up entirely new avenues for the ultra-wealthy to collect rare and exclusive digital assets that were once impossible to own in the traditional sense. NFTs are unique digital items or assets that are stored on a blockchain, allowing them to be bought, sold, and traded as verifiable, one-of-a-kind pieces of content.

In the world of digital art, NFTs have provided a platform for creators to monetize their work in unprecedented ways. Artists like Beeple, whose digital collage "Everydays: The First 5000 Days" sold for $69 million at a Christie's auction in 2021, have brought NFTs into the mainstream. For the ultra-wealthy, purchasing NFTs is not just about acquiring art—it is about embracing a new form of digital ownership and participating in a cutting-edge asset class that holds the potential for both cultural influence and financial appreciation.

In addition to art, NFTs are now being used to represent digital collectibles such as virtual real estate, music, and even luxury fashion. Brands like Gucci and Balenciaga have embraced digital fashion, selling

NFT-based clothing that can be worn in virtual worlds like Decentraland or The Sandbox. For younger collectors, NFTs provide a contemporary take on the exclusive world of art and collectibles, allowing them to participate in a space that is both innovative and lucrative.

Digital collectibles, once seen as a niche of the tech-savvy elite, have quickly become a significant part of the luxury collecting world. Whether it's rare digital artworks, virtual sneakers, or NFTs tied to physical goods, the market for digital collectibles is rapidly growing, attracting wealthy buyers eager to own unique pieces that transcend the physical world.

## Concluding thoughts

The world of art, collectibles, and luxury hobbies has become an essential element of the 21st century's culture of wealth and status. From contemporary art as an investment asset to the pursuit of exclusive hobbies like yachting and car racing, today's ultra-wealthy are not just buying products; they are investing in experiences and status. The rise of NFTs and digital collectibles has opened up an entirely new chapter in the world of luxury, offering both young and old collectors unique ways to engage with art and exclusivity in a modern, digital space.

As the luxury market continues to evolve, the boundaries between physical and digital worlds will blur, with high-end hobbies, exclusive art, and cutting-edge collectibles representing not just a symbol of wealth but a new era in which luxury, identity, and investment intersect in increasingly innovative and immersive ways.

## Chapter 3.6: Technology and the Luxury Lifestyle

As the world becomes increasingly interconnected and technology continues to shape every aspect of daily life, the luxury market has adapted and evolved to meet the demands of a new generation of consumers.

These consumers, often referred to as "digital natives," are not only seeking the finest products and services, but they also expect those offerings to be personalized, technologically advanced, and deeply integrated with their digital lives. From personalized shopping experiences driven by data insights to the use of wearable technology that signifies both status and tech-savviness, technology is deeply embedded within the luxury lifestyle.

In this chapter, we will explore how the rise of data-driven insights has revolutionized the luxury sector, enabling brands to offer tailor-made experiences that cater to individual tastes. We will also delve into the world of wearable technology, which has evolved beyond fitness trackers and smartwatches to become a status symbol of exclusivity and technological sophistication. Finally, we will examine the growth of digital exclusivity, including the rise of members-only digital platforms and online luxury clubs that offer their clientele exclusive access to high-end experiences, products, and services in the digital realm. These platforms provide a new layer of exclusivity, making luxury more accessible but still firmly reserved for the elite.

## Personalized Luxury Through Data-Driven Insights

The concept of personalization in luxury is not new, but in recent years, it has been taken to an entirely new level through the application of data analytics and artificial intelligence (AI). As luxury brands strive to offer experiences that feel more bespoke and unique to each individual, data is used to enhance every interaction, making the luxury experience more intuitive and personalized than ever before.

## Tailored Shopping Recommendations

One of the most prominent ways in which luxury brands are using data is through personalized shopping experiences. Companies such as

Net-a-Porter, Farfetch, and Burberry have integrated AI and machine learning algorithms to analyze customers' purchasing history, browsing patterns, and even their social media activity. By using this data, these brands can provide personalized product recommendations and create targeted advertisements that feel tailor-made for each customer.

For example, Net-a-Porter, an online retailer for luxury fashion, uses an AI-powered algorithm to offer personalized shopping suggestions based on a customer's previous purchases and browsing history. The platform even adjusts product recommendations as it gathers more data, ensuring that the customer is continuously presented with items that reflect their evolving tastes and preferences. Similarly, Farfetch leverages data-driven insights to deliver a curated selection of high-end fashion items that are customized to each shopper's individual style, further enhancing the personalized shopping experience.

Additionally, data allows for customized products, where buyers can create one-of-a-kind items that match their personal preferences. Brands including Louis Vuitton and Gucci have embraced this approach, offering customization options for items like luggage, shoes, and even handbags. Customers can now select the colors, materials, and finishes of their products, ensuring that the final result is not just a product, but an expression of personal style.

## Virtual Personal Shoppers

To further enhance the level of personalization, some luxury retailers have begun offering virtual personal shoppers. Powered by AI chatbots and augmented reality (AR), these virtual assistants help clients navigate their shopping experience and provide real-time recommendations. For example, Chanel has integrated an AI-powered stylist feature on its online platform that allows customers to receive tailored product suggestions based on their style profile. This personalized digital service ensures that even online shopping can mirror the bespoke service one would receive in a high-end boutique, blending technology with luxury service.

Moreover, high-end department stores like Harrods and Neiman Marcus are using data-driven insights to provide a more personal touch. Their concierge services are now accessible via apps, where clients can book appointments, request custom products, or get personalized recommendations on everything from fashion to interior design. This emphasis on customer intimacy and personalized experiences is now a hallmark of the luxury market, reflecting the growing importance of providing not just products, but experiences tailored to the individual's preferences.

## Wearable Technology and Status Symbols

Wearable technology has moved far beyond simple fitness trackers and smartwatches. Today, these devices serve not only as tools for health tracking and communication, but also as luxury status symbols, signifying a blend of tech-savviness and exclusivity. The integration of wearables into the luxury lifestyle has redefined how affluent individuals display their wealth, and it is reshaping the way we view personal accessories.

## The Apple Watch: A Tech and Fashion Statement

The Apple Watch, once viewed primarily as a piece of wearable technology, has quickly become a luxury item for the tech-savvy elite. The release of the Apple Watch Edition, featuring a 24-karat gold case, signaled a shift toward positioning smartwatches as a new form of luxury accessory. With its sleek design and a price tag that started at $10,000, the Apple Watch Edition symbolized exclusivity, luxury, and status.

Although the gold edition has since been discontinued, Apple has continued to cater to the luxury market with the Apple Watch Ultra—a high-end, rugged smartwatch designed for athletes and explorers, priced at $799 and offering features including enhanced durability, longer battery life, and advanced GPS tracking. For the affluent consumer, the Apple Watch Ultra is not just a functional tool, but a statement. It has become an accessory that pairs seamlessly with other luxury items, elevating both personal style and the experience of owning the latest, cutting-edge technology.

## Custom Headphones and Augmented Reality

Another example of wearables becoming integral to the luxury lifestyle is the demand for custom headphones and augmented reality (AR) devices. Companies like Bang & Olufsen and Sennheiser offer high-end, customizable audio equipment that caters to those who seek superior quality and design. For example, Bang & Olufsen's Beoplay headphones, often priced over $500, combine exceptional sound quality with a sleek, minimalist design, making them a popular choice for consumers seeking both luxury and performance. Similarly, Master & Dynamic produces high-end headphones, with models that can exceed $1,000, offering superior materials like leather and stainless steel, along with audiophile-quality sound. These premium headphones have become much more than just a tech product; they have become a luxury accessory and a status symbol in their own right.

In the world of augmented reality (AR) devices, both Microsoft and Apple are pushing the boundaries of what is possible with smart glasses and other wearable tech. Apple's Vision Pro headset, for instance, was unveiled as an ultra-luxury AR product that combines virtual and augmented reality in a sleek, sophisticated design. With a price tag of $3,499, the Vision Pro is expected to become a luxury item that appeals to both tech enthusiasts and those seeking the next big thing in wearable technology.

These wearable luxury items are not only about providing functional benefits, but about aligning their owners with the values of exclusivity, sophistication, and technological prowess. For many affluent consumers, wearing these items is as much about showing the world their status and access to cutting-edge tech as it is about the products' actual functionality.

## Digital Exclusivity and Members-Only Platforms

The luxury market is increasingly shifting from traditional brick-and-mortar experiences to the digital realm, with online luxury clubs and members-only platforms offering exclusive access to products, services, and experiences that were once only available to those with physical access to high-end boutiques and exclusive events. These digital platforms represent a new era of luxury exclusivity, where wealth and access to rare items are curated through online communities, turning digital platforms into elite spaces for the ultra-wealthy.

## Online Luxury Clubs

One such example of digital exclusivity is The Net-A-Porter Collective, a members-only shopping platform launched by the high-end online retailer. This exclusive platform allows select clients to access limited-edition collections, attend private fashion events, and receive personalized styling services. Similarly, Farfetch has introduced a Private Client service for its most affluent customers, offering them early access to luxury collections, private shopping experiences, and personalized concierge services. These platforms offer a level of personalized service that reflects the growing desire for luxury in the digital space, where exclusivity is maintained through curated access and the promise of one-of-a-kind experiences.

The rise of private members-only communities such as Soho House and The Wing has also played a role in shaping the modern luxury experience. These exclusive, often invitation-only spaces, both physical and digital, cater to an affluent clientele seeking networking opportunities, discreet socializing, and access to high-end events and private experiences. The ability to gain entry to these exclusive platforms signals social status and offers a space where connections can be made in an environment that values privacy, exclusivity, and cultural cachet.

## Digital Platforms for Rare Products and Services

In addition to online shopping clubs, digital exclusivity has also found its way into luxury event planning, product launches, and the sale of rare items. Hermès and Gucci have embraced online-exclusive releases to target the digitally native luxury consumer. Limited-edition items and collaborations between high-end brands and renowned artists are increasingly available only through members-only digital platforms, increasing their perceived value by limiting access.

A great example of this is the Gucci Vault, a digital platform that offers exclusive digital collectibles and access to rare physical products. The platform allows members to purchase items and attend exclusive events, further emphasizing the growing influence of digital luxury. Similarly, Clubhouse—a private, invite-only social audio platform—has become an exclusive digital space where members can gain access to curated events, conversations with high-profile figures, and discussions on topics ranging from business and finance to luxury fashion and art.

## Concluding thoughts

Technology has seamlessly integrated itself into the world of luxury lifestyle, reshaping the way consumers experience and express their wealth. From data-driven insights that create deeply personalized shopping experiences to wearable technology that signifies both sophistication and exclusivity, the luxury market is being redefined by innovations that blend traditional luxury with cutting-edge tech. Additionally, the rise of digital exclusivity and members-only platforms has created new ways for the affluent to connect, engage, and consume, making luxury increasingly accessible in the digital realm while maintaining its sense of privilege and exclusivity.

As the luxury market continues to evolve, the integration of technology will undoubtedly play a critical role in shaping the future of luxury experiences, transforming the very definition of what it means to live a luxurious lifestyle in the 21st century.

# Chapter 3.7: High-End Wellness and Health as the New Luxury

In today's world, luxury is evolving beyond designer labels, private jets, and dream vacations. Now, for the wealthiest among us, true luxury includes investing in health, wellness, and longevity. Instead of just acquiring things, the affluent are seeking ways to live longer, healthier, and more balanced lives. This chapter dives into three big areas where wellness and health are becoming the new symbols of luxury: exclusive wellness retreats, personalized healthcare through medical concierge services, and the rise of biohacking and anti-aging technology.

## Luxury Wellness Retreats and Clinics

Not long ago, the idea of luxury meant taking a fancy trip to a well-known destination or staying in a five-star resort. Now, affluent travelers want more—they want an experience that leaves them feeling renewed and healthier. That's where luxury wellness retreats come in. These exclusive destinations are about more than just relaxation; they're designed to recharge the mind, body, and spirit, offering custom wellness programs that focus on total rejuvenation.

Take SHA Wellness Clinic in Spain, for example. It's a high-end wellness destination where Western medicine meets Eastern holistic practices, offering everything from acupuncture to DNA analysis. Here, guests aren't just signing up for massages and facials; they're undergoing a health overhaul, with programs tailored to specific goals like detox, weight loss, and stress management. And, of course, this all takes place with stunning views of the Mediterranean, creating an experience that feels luxurious in every sense.

Holistic health has become a key part of the luxury wellness trend. Luxury retreats go beyond the typical spa day and offer services like private yoga sessions, meditation, and sound therapy—practices that help clients find balance and inner peace. Aman Resorts, which operates worldwide in breathtaking destinations from Bali to Bhutan, is a perfect example. Their Aman Wellness experiences offer healing rituals, energy treatments, and even life-coaching services that help guests reconnect with themselves, all within ultra-luxurious settings.

As an executive at Aman commented, "Individuals are now seeking deeper relaxation and a more integrated approach to address the root cause of their stress, may it be structural, lifestyle or emotionally generated, which is what our new wellness concept is based on."

Nutrition is also getting the VIP treatment. Many wellness retreats now include bespoke nutrition plans tailored to each individual. At The Ranch Malibu in California, for example, guests enjoy plant-based meals designed to fuel their bodies without any processed sugars, caffeine, alcohol, or dairy. These menus aren't just about being "healthy"; they're customized to optimize performance and wellness, leaving guests feeling cleansed, re-energized, and ready to take on the world again.

In short, luxury wellness retreats have redefined what it means to indulge. For the wealthy, these retreats are an investment in both physical and mental well-being. Instead of just checking out for a few days, they're checking in with their health, prioritizing long-term vitality, and experiencing the idea of luxury in a completely new way.

## Medical Concierge Services and Personalized Healthcare

Today, luxury goes hand-in-hand with personal healthcare. High-net-worth individuals are increasingly turning to medical concierge services that offer them around-the-clock access to doctors, same-day appointments, and customized health plans. These services promise a hassle-free, high-end healthcare experience, giving the affluent a direct line to world-class doctors without the usual obstacles like long wait times and insurance restrictions.

Medical concierge services provide a level of personal attention that's nearly unheard of in regular healthcare. For example, Private Medical, based in Los Angeles, has built its reputation on delivering continuous, preventive, and personalized care. Their team handles everything from routine visits to highly specialized treatments, all with a focus on identifying and addressing health issues before they become serious. They even connect clients with renowned specialists if needed, ensuring they're always receiving the best care available.

Similarly, the Cleveland Clinic's Concierge Medicine program offers a luxury healthcare experience within one of the most prestigious medical institutions in the world. Patients get exclusive amenities, one-on-one consultations with top doctors, and personalized health assessments. The goal is to create a health plan that takes a holistic view of each patient's wellness, going beyond just treating symptoms to focus on preventive care. These programs include services like genetic testing, giving patients insight into their own health risks and empowering them to make proactive choices.

Concierge medicine also caters to the mental health needs of the wealthy, who face their own unique set of stressors. Dr. Daniel Amen's clinics, for example, specialize in brain health and mental well-being, using neuroimaging to create custom treatment plans. This approach helps clients manage stress, enhance focus, and improve memory, giving them tools to handle the pressures of high-powered lifestyles with confidence.

Affluent clients are also gaining access to breakthrough medical treatments that aren't widely available. Stem cell therapy, for instance, has become a popular option for those looking for regenerative and anti-aging benefits. Once only accessible to researchers and specialists, these treatments are now offered in select high-end clinics, providing clients with advanced medical options that could enhance their quality of life and extend their health span.

For those with the means, these personalized healthcare services offer a level of security and convenience that's become a critical part of their lifestyle. Health is seen as an investment, and being able to access the latest medical advancements and enjoy a tailored health experience is now a symbol of true luxury. It's a reminder that luxury today isn't just about material wealth—it's also about the freedom to live a long, healthy, and fulfilling life.

## Biohacking and Anti-Aging Innovations

Thanks to advancements in technology, a whole new world of personal enhancement, longevity, and anti-aging solutions is opening up, and affluent consumers are diving in. Biohacking—using science and tech to optimize the body and mind—has become particularly popular, with wealthy individuals investing in everything from genetic testing to wearable health trackers, all in the pursuit of better performance and a longer, healthier life.

Biohacking includes a wide range of practices, from lifestyle tweaks to medical interventions. Genetic testing is one area that's booming, with companies like 23andMe offering insights into health risks and even dietary preferences. But luxury clients often prefer more specialized services like those provided by the Health Nucleus clinic, where clients get a comprehensive look at their genetic and physical health through full-genome sequencing and advanced medical imaging. This in-depth information allows them to take a proactive approach to longevity and wellness.

Wearable devices are another staple in the biohacking toolkit. The Oura Ring, for example, monitors sleep, heart rate, and activity, giving users insights they can use to fine-tune their daily routines for optimal health. This concept of "self-quantification" is growing, as more affluent individuals use technology to track and improve their health. These devices aren't just about fitness; they're about achieving a higher level of self-awareness and performance.

Anti-aging treatments are also central to this trend. The wealthy are investing in treatments like NAD+ therapy, which is said to combat cellular aging, and exosome therapy, which supports tissue repair. These are the types of advanced therapies typically found in luxury clinics, attracting clients who want to extend their health span as well as their lifespan.

Cryotherapy, known for its benefits in reducing inflammation, promoting collagen production, and helping with athletic recovery, is another popular choice among affluent clients. The iCRYO facilities in the U.S., for instance, offer cryotherapy as part of their wellness offerings, providing a way for clients to maintain cellular health and stay youthful, all while enjoying a comfortable, high-end setting.

Hormone optimization treatments are another way biohacking is entering the luxury sector. Many clinics now offer hormone panels and bioidentical hormone treatments, designed to keep clients feeling energetic and youthful even as they age. This approach is especially popular among those in their middle age who want to maintain vitality and continue enjoying a dynamic lifestyle.

For high-net-worth individuals, biohacking isn't just about health— it's about control and empowerment. By investing in biohacking and anti-aging innovations, they're taking charge of their longevity and vitality, ensuring that they can continue to enjoy the fruits of their success for as long as possible. In today's luxury landscape, health and wellness are seen as the ultimate assets, and tools like biohacking provide a path to maximize those assets to the fullest.

## Concluding thoughts

To sum it up, luxury today is being redefined by health and wellness. Wealthy individuals are no longer just acquiring possessions; they're investing in their own health, longevity, and personal optimization. From exclusive wellness retreats to personalized healthcare services and biohacking innovations, the affluent are embracing a lifestyle that prioritizes well-being. It's a reminder that true luxury is about living well, and for today's elite, that means a life filled with health, balance, and vitality.

# Chapter 3.8: The Resurgence of Luxury Cars and Private Transportation

In the world of high-end lifestyles, luxury vehicles and private modes of transportation are experiencing a renaissance. But this isn't about just fast cars or exclusive jets; it's about how these modes of transportation are evolving to reflect modern values, including sustainability, tech innovation, and convenience. For the wealthy, getting from point A to point B is no longer just a journey; it's a statement. In this chapter, we'll explore how luxury cars are adapting to a more eco-conscious world, how private jets, yachts, and helicopters have become symbols of freedom and flexibility, and how autonomous and AI-powered luxury vehicles are shaping the future of luxury on wheels.

## The Evolution of the Luxury Car Market

Today's luxury car market is in a state of transformation. For years, luxury cars were known for powerful engines, iconic designs, and, let's face it, not exactly being eco-friendly. But as the world shifts towards sustainability, even high-end automakers are changing their approach. Now, luxury isn't just about exclusivity and performance; it's also about being eco-conscious, and the wealthiest buyers are more interested than ever in vehicles that reflect these values.

Take Tesla, for instance. While it started as a disruptor in the tech and electric car space, Tesla's high-end models quickly became a staple among affluent drivers who wanted a luxury car that also happened to be electric. The Tesla Model S Plaid, for instance, boasts a zero-to-sixty acceleration of under two seconds, rivaling the world's most iconic sports cars. But beyond speed, it's a status symbol of eco-conscious wealth. Driving a Tesla—or better yet, pulling up in the ultra-exclusive Model X with falcon-wing doors—shows an alignment with sustainability that's appealing to the modern luxury consumer.

But it's not just Tesla that's making waves. Traditional luxury brands Mercedes-Benz, Porsche, and even Bentley are rolling out electric and hybrid models that blend eco-responsibility with pure luxury. Mercedes-Benz's EQS, for instance, is a fully electric luxury sedan that offers all the elegance and cutting-edge tech one would expect from the brand. With a sleek design, whisper-quiet ride, and high-tech features, the EQS is redefining what it means to drive a luxury car. For many, it's the best of both worlds: they're driving a vehicle that's both responsible and luxurious, without sacrificing style or performance.

Even brands traditionally associated with high-powered gasoline engines, like Lamborghini and Ferrari, are shifting gears. Ferrari has launched the SF90 Stradale, its first plug-in hybrid supercar, which merges the unmistakable Ferrari roar with an electric boost that supports performance while addressing eco-conscious concerns. Meanwhile, Lamborghini is working on hybrid versions of its iconic models, signaling that even the most exclusive automakers are recognizing the importance of sustainable luxury. These vehicles show that the wealthy don't have to choose between status and responsibility—they can have both.

This new breed of luxury car is more than a vehicle; it's a message. For affluent drivers, these eco-conscious cars represent not only wealth but also a commitment to a sustainable future. They're still status symbols, but now they tell a story of innovation, responsibility, and exclusivity, wrapped up in one sleek, high-performance package.

## Private Jets, Yachts, and Helicopters

When it comes to private transportation, it's hard to ignore the allure of personal jets, yachts, and helicopters. While these modes of transport have always been symbols of wealth and power, they're now more than just ways to avoid long lines at the airport or cruise in style. Today, they represent a lifestyle of ultimate freedom and flexibility—a kind of private world where time, convenience, and personal space are the ultimate luxuries.

Take private jets, for example. They've seen a surge in popularity, especially with the rise of private jet memberships and fractional ownership. Companies including NetJets and Wheels Up allow members to access private jet services without owning the aircraft outright. Instead, members pay for a share or hours of use, offering the flexibility of private travel without the full responsibility of ownership. For high-net-worth individuals, this means they can have the perks of private air travel—skipping commercial terminals, traveling on their own schedule, and enjoying onboard luxury—without the hassle of maintenance and management.

Costs for jet cards vary by provider but typically start around $150,000 for 25 hours on a light jet, with larger jets costing significantly more. Fractional ownership, similar to a timeshare, allows multiple people to own shares of a jet, lowering upfront costs while still providing flexibility. However, shareholders are still responsible for their portion of the operating and maintenance costs, which are billed monthly and add up quickly.

In a way, private jet memberships have democratized private aviation for the ultra-wealthy, making it more accessible and more flexible than ever.

Then there's the yacht market, which has evolved from simple vessels of leisure to ultra-luxurious, custom-built floating palaces. Today's superyachts are masterpieces of design, often equipped with amenities that rival five-star hotels: think infinity pools, onboard spas, private theaters, and even helipads. Companies like Feadship and Lürssen are renowned for their custom builds, creating yachts that cater to each owner's unique vision and taste. The Serene, a superyacht owned by a Saudi prince, is complete with multiple pools, jacuzzis, and even a saltwater swimming pool. For owners, these yachts aren't just boats; they're private islands on the water, a symbol of their power and freedom to roam the seas on their terms.

Personal helicopters are also becoming more popular among the elite, particularly as urban traffic congestion grows. Helicopters provide the ultimate convenience for short-distance travel, allowing owners to hop between city centers, estates, and even nearby islands without getting stuck in traffic. Brands like Sikorsky and Bell are leading the way in luxury helicopters, offering models that are as comfortable and stylish as they are practical. Some wealthy individuals are even integrating helipads directly into their homes or yachts, creating seamless transitions between different modes of private transportation.

In short, private transportation is more than a way to get from one place to another—it's a lifestyle. With private jets, yachts, and helicopters, the wealthy can tailor every aspect of their journey to their preferences, schedule, and style. This level of control and convenience is a defining feature of luxury today, giving them the freedom to navigate the world on their own terms.

## Autonomous and AI-Powered Luxury Vehicles

The future of luxury transportation is being shaped by advances in artificial intelligence and autonomous driving, and high-end automakers are leading the charge. Imagine stepping into a car that recognizes you, adjusts the seats and climate to your preferences, plays your favorite playlist, and can drive itself. For the wealthy, this is no longer a futuristic fantasy—it's becoming a reality.

Luxury brands like BMW, Audi, and Mercedes-Benz are already offering high-tech amenities powered by AI, creating a driving experience that's not just about comfort but personalization. For instance, Mercedes-Benz's EQS features a system that uses AI to "learn" driver preferences over time, making the experience increasingly tailored and intuitive. The MBUX Hyperscreen, an expansive, curved digital dashboard, is designed to respond to both touch and voice commands, allowing drivers and passengers to control nearly every aspect of the vehicle without lifting a finger. The car adapts to the driver's preferences, whether it's remembering their preferred route, adjusting the seat settings, or knowing which music they like during a night drive.

Meanwhile, Cadillac has introduced the Super Cruise feature in its luxury models, offering one of the closest experiences to hands-free driving currently available. Super Cruise uses cameras, radar, and advanced mapping data to enable a semi-autonomous driving experience on compatible highways. The driver can take their hands off the wheel and let the car take over, making it ideal for long-distance travel. Tesla's Autopilot is also a well-known example, with features like lane centering, adaptive cruise control, and even "Summon," which allows the car to drive itself to the owner in a parking lot. This technology isn't perfect yet, but it's rapidly advancing, and it's clear that luxury brands are betting on a future where high-end cars drive themselves.

The next step? Full autonomy. Brands like Rolls-Royce and Bentley are exploring how fully autonomous driving could transform the luxury experience even further. Imagine a Bentley that could drive itself to pick up a client or a Rolls-Royce that could take the owner home after an evening out, offering the ultimate chauffeur experience without an actual driver. For the wealthy, this technology represents more than just convenience; it's a way to own a vehicle that's intelligent, efficient, and utterly luxurious.

The rise of autonomous luxury cars also opens the door for personalization like never before. With the driver free to relax, entertain, or even work in the back seat, car interiors are being reimagined to accommodate these new possibilities. Companies are designing cabins that feel more like private lounges or mini-offices, complete with reclining seats, state-of-the-art entertainment systems, and connectivity options that turn the car into a mobile workspace or retreat. The concept of the "third space"—a space that's not home or work, but a hybrid of both—is becoming a central theme in luxury car design, allowing owners to make the most of every moment they spend on the road.

In this world of AI-powered, self-driving luxury, the car becomes more than just transportation—it becomes an extension of the owner's lifestyle. Whether they're focused on relaxation, productivity, or pure enjoyment, the car adapts to their needs, offering a futuristic and highly personalized experience that reflects the ultimate in modern luxury.

## Concluding thoughts:

The world of luxury transportation is expanding in remarkable ways. From eco-friendly electric cars that offer style without sacrificing sustainability, to private jets and yachts that provide unparalleled freedom, to AI-driven vehicles that bring the future to the present, the wealthy now have more options than ever to travel in ways that reflect their values, priorities, and tastes. In this new era, luxury isn't just about getting from place to place—it's about doing so with intention, personalization, and a commitment to living life at the highest level.

## Chapter 3.9: Luxury in Media and Entertainment

The way we consume media and entertainment has changed dramatically over the years. For the affluent, this shift isn't just about keeping up with trends; it's about enjoying these experiences in a way that feels personal, exclusive, and deeply tailored to their tastes. From niche streaming services and private theaters to high-end gaming and virtual reality, the world of luxury entertainment is expanding and redefining what it means to experience media.

### Exclusive Streaming and Curated Content

With the explosion of streaming services in recent years, it might seem like every possible niche is already covered. But for affluent audiences, mainstream platforms like Netflix, Disney+, or HBO Max often fall short in providing the highly curated and exclusive experiences they're after. Enter a new wave of streaming services that cater specifically to the tastes and preferences of high-net-worth individuals, offering exclusive, curated content that's designed to appeal to their unique lifestyle.

One example of this is MUBI, a curated streaming service that focuses on classic and independent films. For film lovers with refined tastes, MUBI isn't just another streaming service; it's a destination for high-quality cinema that's carefully selected by experts. Instead of offering a seemingly endless array of choices, MUBI features a rotating selection of handpicked films each month. This curated approach has a certain appeal for viewers who prefer fewer options but with a guarantee of quality, allowing them to experience cinema as an art form rather than mere entertainment.

Another platform, CuriosityStream, offers documentaries and educational content across topics including science, technology, history, and nature. Created by John Hendricks, founder of the Discovery Channel, CuriosityStream has been crafted for viewers who crave intelligent content and want to learn more about the world in an enriching way. For wealthy viewers who value knowledge, platforms like CuriosityStream provide an immersive, upscale way to explore topics that align with their interests.

Private media services have also emerged, offering content that's available only to select clients. One notable example is The Screening Room, an exclusive service that allows members to watch newly released films in the comfort of their own homes, often on the same day these films hit theaters. Originally targeted at high-net-worth individuals and families, The Screening Room's approach to streaming lets users avoid the hassle of public theaters, offering first-run movies directly to their homes. This exclusivity resonates with wealthy audiences who prioritize privacy and convenience.

Beyond the platforms themselves, the concept of bespoke content curation is taking off. Services like Criterion Channel offer expertly curated collections of films, often based on directors, genres, or themes, catering to those with an appreciation for cinematic history. Wealthy viewers can dive into selections that have been carefully organized to provide a more enriched viewing experience, creating an atmosphere similar to browsing a private library of films.

For the affluent, media consumption is as much about the experience as it is about the content itself. These niche streaming services and private media options reflect a desire for exclusivity, sophistication, and a connection to the arts that goes beyond mainstream entertainment. The act of watching a film, documentary, or series becomes a luxurious experience that fits seamlessly into their elevated lifestyle.

## High-End Gaming and Virtual Reality

Luxury isn't just about exclusive films or curated content; it's also extending to the world of gaming and virtual reality, where affluent individuals are finding new ways to immerse themselves in digital worlds. High-end VR setups, exclusive gaming memberships, and luxury-themed virtual environments have created a new realm where aspirational living meets advanced technology. For many wealthy gamers, these immersive experiences are a modern form of escapism, one where they can enjoy the thrill of exploration, competition, and connection in entirely new ways.

VR gaming has come a long way from its early days, and now luxury VR systems like the Varjo XR-3 and HTC Vive Pro 2 offer the highest levels of immersion and clarity on the market. These setups provide ultra-high-definition visuals and motion tracking that make virtual worlds feel almost as real as the physical world. For affluent users who can afford the best in VR technology, these systems offer a level of quality that most casual gamers never experience, bringing the virtual world to life in a way that's immersive, thrilling, and completely transporting.

The concept of exclusive gaming memberships is also taking off, with services such as Parsec Arcade and Shadow offering access to high-performance gaming without the need for a physical gaming console. These cloud-based platforms provide access to powerful gaming setups remotely, allowing users to experience top-notch gaming experiences from virtually any device. For luxury-minded gamers, the convenience and exclusivity of these services are a major draw, offering access to a "gamer's paradise" without the need for hardware.

Luxury gaming isn't limited to VR or cloud-based setups; virtual worlds themselves are evolving to include luxury elements. Roblox and Fortnite, for instance, have introduced high-fashion brands like Gucci and Balenciaga into their digital landscapes. Virtual items, once seen as gimmicks, are now becoming status symbols, with limited-edition "skins" or outfits that players can buy, often for hundreds or even thousands of dollars. For the wealthy, buying these digital goods is an extension of their real-world preferences—where the brand names they wear in real life are mirrored in their digital identities.

We're also seeing a rise in virtual spaces that mimic luxury real estate. Platforms like Decentraland allow users to buy, design, and sell digital real estate within a virtual world, creating exclusive, upscale environments where they can socialize, relax, or host events. Some wealthy users have even commissioned custom-built virtual mansions complete with pools, private theaters, and landscaped gardens. These spaces aren't just for showing off—they're used for private gatherings, gaming parties, and even as a space to host virtual meetings, blending entertainment with functionality in an entirely new way.

For those with a taste for both gaming and luxury, these immersive digital experiences represent a new form of aspirational living. They're spaces where imagination meets exclusivity, allowing affluent users to explore worlds where they can be whoever they want and own whatever they desire. High-end gaming and virtual reality are no longer just a pastime; they're a way for the wealthy to engage with technology in a personal, creative, and highly exclusive way.

## Luxury Cinemas and Private Film Screenings

The love for cinema is universal, but the way the wealthy experience it is anything but ordinary. For high-net-worth individuals, going to the movies doesn't mean standing in line for tickets and hoping for a good seat. Instead, it's an elevated experience, often in luxury theaters that rival the finest hotel lounges, with gourmet food, private screening rooms, and high-end seating that turns movie-going into an indulgent event.

One example of luxury cinema done right is iPic Theaters. Known for their plush recliners, personal blankets, and pillows, iPic takes the movie experience to the next level. Each seat has a call button that lets viewers order cocktails, wine, and gourmet snacks directly from their seats, with a menu crafted by professional chefs. For the wealthy, these theaters offer a place to relax and enjoy a film in an environment that's as comfortable as their own living room but with the added thrill of a night out.

Then there's The Everyman Cinemas in the UK, a chain of luxury theaters that offer an intimate, premium viewing experience. These theaters feature cozy sofas, waiter service, and a menu that includes everything from artisanal pizzas to gourmet popcorn. It's a far cry from the typical cinema experience and is designed to feel like a sophisticated lounge rather than a traditional theater. For high-net-worth moviegoers, Everyman offers the opportunity to watch a film in a way that feels upscale, relaxed, and perfectly tailored to their lifestyle.

For those who prefer watching films in the privacy of their own homes, luxury home theaters are also on the rise. The wealthy are investing in custom-built home theaters that offer the ultimate in exclusivity and privacy. These private cinemas are often equipped with cutting-edge audio-visual technology, soundproofing, and designer interiors that feel as luxurious as the movie palaces of old. Companies like Kaleidescape offer high-end home theater systems that let users stream or download films in cinema-quality formats, making the home viewing experience truly exceptional. Some ultra-luxury home theaters even include cinema-grade projectors and screens, reclining leather seats, and concessions areas that mimic the theater experience.

Private film screenings are another indulgence that's gaining popularity among affluent audiences. Some individuals and families host private screenings for friends and guests, often selecting films that haven't yet been widely released. Companies such as The Screening Room provide access to first-run movies in the comfort of one's home theater, letting clients skip the public theater altogether. Hosting private screenings has become a way for wealthy individuals to share their love for film in an intimate, exclusive setting, whether it's for a special occasion or just a cozy night with friends.

For the affluent, cinema isn't just about watching a movie—it's about creating an experience. Whether they're at a luxury theater or in their own custom-built screening room, the goal is to enjoy the film in a way that feels intimate, comfortable, and deeply personal. High-end cinema experiences reflect a love for storytelling and artistry, but with a preference for privacy, exclusivity, and indulgence that only the wealthiest can afford.

## Concluding thoughts:

The world of luxury media and entertainment is transforming how affluent individuals consume content. From exclusive streaming platforms and high-end gaming setups to luxury cinemas and private screenings, these experiences offer something more than just entertainment—they provide a sense of exclusivity, personalization, and indulgence that aligns with the elevated lifestyle of the wealthy. For the affluent, media and entertainment have become more than just a pastime; they're an opportunity to experience culture, artistry, and technology in ways that are deeply satisfying and tailored to their unique tastes. In this era, true luxury in media and entertainment is about curating a world of experiences that can be enjoyed in private, on their own terms.

# Chapter 3.10 Love and Luxury: The Dynamics of Dating Among the Ultra-Affluent

## The Role of Exclusivity and Trust in Affluent Relationships

For the ultra-affluent, dating isn't simply a matter of companionship or romance. It's about finding someone who fits into a unique lifestyle marked by luxury, discretion, and often complex personal and financial stakes. This elite group approaches dating with a set of expectations and priorities that reflect their high-profile lives.

For instance, Stephen, a private equity executive from New York, notes that "you can't just date anyone in my position; it's not about being elitist—it's about finding someone who understands the nuances." Stephen's need for someone who respects his lifestyle and privacy is shared by many in his circle, where trust becomes the foundation of all relationships.

In addition to trust, discretion is essential. Ultra-affluent individuals often live under intense scrutiny—whether from the media, business circles, or the public. Many wealthy individuals find that dating within a close-knit social network or using exclusive matchmaking services allows them to maintain their privacy and reputation.

## Matchmaking as a Bespoke Service

Exclusive matchmaking services have become a go-to resource for affluent singles. These services offer more than just matches; they offer the promise of discretion, compatibility, and curated connections. Kelleher International, for example, is a leading matchmaking service known for its bespoke approach to connecting high-net-worth individuals.

For the ultra-high-net-worth client who demands nothing less than the finest, Kelleher's matchmaking services start at $30,000 for a focused local search and can exceed $300,000 for a global hunt. It's a uniquely tailored experience that aligns with the needs of those with extremely high standards and limited time.

One of Kelleher's clients, Maria, a CEO in the tech industry, explains why she opted for the service. "I don't have time to go on countless dates, and I wanted someone who matched my ambition and lifestyle." Kelleher's team understood Maria's criteria: they conducted background checks and personality assessments to ensure any match would be compatible with her values and goals.

Another matchmaking service, SEI Club, takes things even further, catering to a more exclusive, global clientele. A client in London, a prominent financier, used SEI to find someone who not only shared his passion for art and philanthropy but also appreciated the demands of his career. SEI's vetting process ensured that every potential match respected his need for privacy. "It's not just about finding someone attractive or interesting," he shared. "It's about finding someone who 'gets' this life."

## Social Networks as Natural Dating Venues

For many affluent singles, the most organic way to meet a compatible partner is through their existing social circles. High-profile charity events, art auctions, private galas, and industry gatherings serve as natural dating venues, where wealthy individuals can connect with others who share similar values and lifestyles.

An example of this is Lauren, a gallery owner, who met her husband, Andrew, at Art Basel in Miami, one of the most exclusive art fairs in the world. "It wasn't just his taste in art; it was his understanding of the lifestyle," Lauren recalls. Both Lauren and Andrew moved in the same circles, attending the same events, and supporting similar philanthropic causes. They had shared experiences and networks, which created a natural connection that was hard to replicate outside these circles.

Similarly, private members-only clubs—such as Soho House, Core Club, and Norwood—are popular spots for dating. These venues serve as a kind of safe haven where affluent singles can relax and socialize without the worry of being scrutinized. In the words of Ryan, a venture capitalist and Core Club member, "It's just easier to be yourself when you're among people who understand your world. You don't have to explain why you're stressed about a board meeting or an investment." Many high-net-worth individuals find dating within these spaces to be far more comfortable and authentic than traditional dating scenarios.

## Dating Apps for the Wealthy: Technology Meets Exclusivity

Exclusive dating apps designed for the affluent have gained popularity as technology becomes more ingrained in the dating landscape. Platforms like Raya, The League, and Luxy are specifically designed to cater to wealthy individuals, combining digital convenience with exclusivity.

Raya, for instance, is known as the "celebrity dating app" due to its rigorous vetting process, which only admits those with established careers or public influence. Emily, a fashion entrepreneur and Raya user, explains, "On other apps, I felt like I was just another profile, but on Raya, I feel seen and understood." This level of exclusivity and targeted networking provides a safe environment where affluent individuals can engage with like-minded partners.

Applying to an elite dating app like Raya involves submitting a detailed application that is thoroughly vetted before acceptance. Raya's process, requires applicants to link their social media accounts and provide personal information that reflects their professional background, lifestyle, and social connections. Profiles are reviewed by both an algorithm and a committee, who look for individuals with qualities that align with the app's exclusive community standards. Successful applicants often have established careers in fields like entertainment, art, fashion, and entrepreneurship, where a notable online presence or industry reputation helps set them apart.

One key part of the application is linking an Instagram account, allowing reviewers to assess both the applicant's social circle and lifestyle. This connection provides a window into an applicant's status, reach, and how they present themselves online—an essential aspect of appealing to a community rooted in social exclusivity. High-profile followers or verified accounts boost an applicant's chances of acceptance, as they signal influence, which adds to the app's allure.

While anyone can technically apply, insider connections significantly increase the likelihood of acceptance on apps like Raya. Referrals from existing members carry weight in the application process. If a current member recommends a friend or associate, this personal endorsement acts as a vote of confidence, helping new applicants bypass some of the scrutiny that comes with being an unknown entity. In these elite communities, the concept of "vouching" mirrors traditional social circles, where personal connections open doors that might otherwise remain closed.

Referrals are especially valuable for those who may not have a public social media presence. Wealthy singles who prioritize privacy often work in fields like finance or law, where they may lack the high follower count but bring other appealing qualities to the app. For these individuals, a referral from a respected member can be the deciding factor in securing a spot.

The League operates similarly, using LinkedIn profiles to curate an elite user base, ensuring that members are career-oriented and highly educated. Luxy, on the other hand, caters explicitly to high-net-worth individuals, with features like income verification and profile screening. Matthew, a Luxy user and hedge fund manager, appreciates the focus on financial compatibility. "Money may not be everything, but having a similar level of financial independence goes a long way in understanding each other's priorities," he notes.

These apps allow wealthy individuals to meet others who appreciate their unique lifestyles, bridging the gap between traditional dating and the specific needs of the ultra-affluent.

## Experiential Dating: Creating Unique Memories Over Material Gifts

In affluent dating circles, memorable experiences often replace traditional gifts as a way to impress or show affection. Instead of gifting jewelry or luxury items, affluent individuals invest in unique experiences, emphasizing shared memories and adventures over material accumulation.

One illustrative example is Mark, a real estate developer, who took his date Sarah on a private weekend getaway to the Maldives. "I wanted our first date to be unforgettable," Mark recalls. By flying her to a private island and arranging a candle-lit dinner on the beach, Mark created a memory that far outweighed any material gift. This emphasis on experiences reflects a growing trend among the affluent to value personal growth and shared adventures.

In a similar vein, Natasha, a luxury travel advisor, often curates customized travel experiences for her high-net-worth clients. "One client wanted to take his partner on a 'round-the-world' adventure, stopping at the most exclusive properties in each country," Natasha says. The trip involved private jet travel, stays at top-tier resorts, and exclusive events, showcasing how affluent couples prioritize unique, one-of-a-kind experiences as a way to bond and express affection.

## The Influence of Family Expectations and Legacy

For ultra-affluent individuals, family expectations often play a major role in romantic decisions. In cases where family fortunes and legacies are involved, finding a partner who aligns with these values can become a priority. Families with significant assets and longstanding traditions may even pressure heirs to choose partners who share their financial and cultural values.

Take the example of Sarah, an heir to a luxury brand. Sarah's family encouraged her to consider partners who shared an understanding of legacy and wealth management. "My parents didn't necessarily dictate who I should date, but they wanted me to be with someone who understood the stakes of our family's legacy," Sarah explains. This is common among affluent families, where marriage and partnership decisions can affect not just the couple but the entire family's financial structure and public reputation.

In these cases, prenuptial agreements, estate planning discussions, and family trust structures are often prerequisites in serious relationships, making dating a more complex process than it might be for others.

## Financial Compatibility as a Foundation for Lasting Relationships

Financial compatibility is crucial in affluent relationships, often functioning as a primary foundation for a successful partnership. The term "power couple" is frequently used to describe high-net-worth pairs who balance demanding careers and shared financial goals. For these individuals, mutual understanding of wealth management and financial independence can be as significant as romance itself.

John, a CEO, and Lisa, a renowned fashion designer, exemplify this balance. "We both have intense careers, but we also respect each other's financial independence," Lisa shares. For John and Lisa, their mutual respect for each other's accomplishments and financial standing enhances their relationship, allowing them to navigate challenges without the financial friction that sometimes affects couples with differing economic backgrounds.

For many affluent singles, financial compatibility isn't just about wealth—it's about finding someone who shares the same level of ambition, risk tolerance, and lifestyle goals. In affluent dating, money and shared financial goals can be a greater predictor of compatibility than traditional romance indicators, as these values underpin much of their daily life and decision-making.

## The Evolving Age and Compatibility Dynamics

Age dynamics are another notable feature in ultra-affluent dating. It's not uncommon to see significant age gaps, especially in relationships where financial independence allows for a wider range of partner preferences. Relationships with notable age differences are not uncommon, and they are often accepted as normal within affluent circles.

For example, wealthy couples such as Rupert Murdoch and Jerry Hall demonstrate that May-December relationships (with an older partner) are often accepted within affluent communities, especially when both partners bring shared lifestyle values or similar life goals. While age differences can be a factor in any relationship, affluent couples often prioritize lifestyle compatibility, shared experiences, and values over age alone.

In cases where both partners are closer in age, lifestyle alignment remains critical. Wealthy individuals often seek partners who share their personal and professional ambitions, creating relationships built on both attraction and mutual respect for one another's achievements.

## Concluding thoughts

Dating among the ultra-affluent appears to blend modern values with traditional expectations around privacy, financial compatibility, and family legacy. As digital platforms continue to refine the experience of connecting elite singles, and as affluent individuals increasingly prioritize experiences over material wealth, the dating landscape will continue to evolve.

For affluent singles, dating in the coming decade will likely see a deeper integration of technology with exclusivity, more emphasis on shared values and lifestyle compatibility, and a continued appreciation for unique experiences. As they balance the demands of wealth, career, and reputation, affluent individuals will navigate relationships in ways that reflect both their individuality and their desire for meaningful connection in a world of luxury.

# Chapter 3.11: The Social Symbolism of Modern Luxury

Luxury, in today's world, has taken on new meanings and evolved in ways that extend far beyond the ownership of rare and expensive things. For the modern affluent consumer, luxury is about more than wealth—it's about expressing personal values, enjoying memorable experiences, and reinforcing a social identity. In this chapter, we'll dive into how luxury has become a medium for wealthy individuals to project their identity and values, how it's shifting from physical possessions to transformative experiences, and why luxury has once again become a powerful social and cultural symbol.

## Wealth as a Reflection of Personal Values

For today's affluent consumers, luxury isn't simply about possessing the most expensive or exclusive items; it's a form of self-expression. Brands, products, and experiences are selected with purpose, as consumers seek to communicate their personal values and principles. Gone are the days when luxury was defined solely by the materials used or the brand name. Now, luxury often reflects values like sustainability, ethical production, and exclusivity.

Consider Patagonia, a brand that's made environmental responsibility a cornerstone of its identity. Known for its commitment to sustainability, Patagonia appeals to high-net-worth individuals who want to align their purchases with their values. By offering ethically sourced materials and pledging significant funds toward environmental causes, Patagonia has successfully positioned itself as a luxury brand for those who care about the planet. For the wealthy consumer, sporting a Patagonia jacket or bag is more than a fashion choice—it's a way to signal a commitment to environmental sustainability.

Similarly, many luxury car manufacturers are embracing eco-conscious values, appealing to affluent consumers who want to make a statement about their environmental responsibility. Brands like Tesla and Porsche have introduced electric models that not only offer high performance but also reflect a commitment to reducing carbon footprints. Driving a Tesla or a Porsche Taycan, for example, is now as much about signaling eco-consciousness as it is about luxury and style. These vehicles represent a shift in the automotive luxury market toward values that resonate with a generation of affluent consumers who see wealth as a tool for positive change.

The world of fashion is also witnessing a push for ethical production, with brands like Stella McCartney leading the way. Known for her commitment to animal welfare and sustainable practices, McCartney's collections attract a clientele that wants their wardrobe to reflect their ethical values. The label's vegan leather handbags, for instance, have become a favorite among celebrities and wealthy consumers who prioritize sustainability. The choice to wear Stella McCartney is not just about owning a designer bag; it's about aligning oneself with a brand that cares about animals, the environment, and responsible production.

This desire to express values through luxury purchases has even reached the realm of hospitality. Six Senses, a luxury resort chain, is renowned for its eco-conscious design and commitment to local communities. Staying at a Six Senses resort isn't just about relaxing in a beautiful location; it's a statement of support for sustainability, wellness, and community investment. Guests who choose Six Senses are signaling a preference for responsible luxury—a concept that resonates with affluent individuals who want their spending to reflect their principles.

In today's luxury landscape, wealth has become a reflection of personal values. Affluent consumers are not just buying products or experiences; they're making statements about who they are, what they stand for, and how they want to impact the world. Luxury has transformed into a form of self-expression, where the brands and products chosen by the wealthy reveal a great deal about their personal identity and beliefs.

## The Shift from Physical Possessions to Experiences

In the past, wealth was often displayed through the accumulation of physical objects—think grand homes, rare cars, and opulent jewelry. While these items still hold a place in the luxury world, there's a noticeable shift among affluent consumers toward spending on experiences rather than things. Today's luxury is about creating memories, having unique stories to tell, and seeking personal growth rather than accumulating more possessions.

Travel has become one of the primary ways that wealthy individuals indulge in luxury experiences. Aman Resorts is a perfect example of this trend. Known for its secluded and exclusive locations, Aman offers experiences that go beyond typical luxury travel. At Amanjiwo in Indonesia, guests can have a private sunrise experience at the ancient Borobudur temple, a UNESCO World Heritage site, complete with a personal guide and a gourmet breakfast in a peaceful, crowd-free setting. For those who can afford it, this type of experience provides a deep sense of connection with the location, the culture, and the history—far more meaningful than simply owning another piece of property or jewelry.

Adventure travel is another area where affluent individuals are investing in experiences over possessions. Companies like Black Tomato offer bespoke trips to remote and untouched destinations. One of their offerings, "Get Lost," allows clients to be dropped into an unknown location—anywhere from the Amazon rainforest to the Mongolian steppe—where they're challenged to find their way back to civilization, all while being supported by a team of experts. For wealthy travelers, this kind of experience offers personal growth, thrill, and the satisfaction of overcoming a challenge. It's a story they can share, an accomplishment they can reflect on, and a memory they'll carry with them.

Beyond travel, luxury experiences are emerging in art and culture. The affluent are increasingly seeking out exclusive opportunities like private art viewings, backstage tours, and personal interactions with renowned artists or performers. The Venice Biennale, for instance, offers VIP programs for collectors and patrons, providing access to private gallery previews, intimate dinners with artists, and insider tours of the city's art scene. For wealthy individuals, these experiences allow them to immerse themselves in culture and artistry in ways that go beyond simply buying a piece of art.

Even wellness has taken on an experiential dimension in the luxury sector. The Ranch Malibu, a high-end wellness retreat, offers guests a transformative experience focused on physical and mental health. Participants spend a week in a rigorous wellness program that includes hiking, yoga, and plant-based meals. It's not just about relaxation—it's a journey that challenges guests physically, mentally, and emotionally. Affluent consumers are drawn to this type of experience because it leaves them feeling rejuvenated, with a sense of accomplishment and personal growth that's far more valuable than a new luxury item.

This shift from possessions to experiences reflects a change in values. For the modern wealthy, luxury is no longer about what you own; it's about what you've done, where you've been, and how these experiences have shaped you. Memories, stories, and personal growth have become the new markers of wealth, adding a layer of meaning and purpose to the concept of luxury that resonates with today's affluent individuals.

## Luxury as a Social and Cultural Status

Even as luxury becomes more personal and values-driven, it hasn't lost its power as a social symbol. In fact, luxury's role as a marker of social and cultural status is as relevant as ever, with affluent individuals using their choices to signify belonging within elite circles. Whether it's through the brands they wear, the places they travel to, or the causes they support, luxury continues to be a visible badge of success and a statement of belonging within a distinct social hierarchy.

One clear example of luxury as a social marker is the world of high-end fashion. Hermès, Louis Vuitton, and Chanel remain at the top of the luxury hierarchy, with products like the Birkin bag or the LV monogrammed luggage serving as iconic status symbols. These items are not just accessories; they're social cues that convey a certain level of wealth, taste, and sophistication. The exclusivity of these brands, combined with their historic designs, means that owning one of these pieces is more than a fashion choice—it's a statement of one's place within an elite community.

For example Owning a Hermès Birkin is not merely about carrying a handbag—it's a status symbol. The bags are meticulously handcrafted and extremely limited in supply, with some requiring waitlists that can span years. This exclusivity, paired with the brand's association with luxury and heritage, turns the Birkin into a piece of cultural cachet. When someone carries one, it signals not just wealth but also access to a world of sophistication and exclusivity that most people can only admire from afar.

The same can be said for Rolex, which are positioned in the market to emphasize tradition, craftsmanship, and enduring value. Wearing a Rolex often connotes a certain level of success and membership in an elite group that appreciates the intersection of luxury and performance. For instance, a vintage Daytona isn't just a watch—it's a connection to icons like Paul Newman, who epitomized the glamour of success and exclusivity.

Luxury real estate is another area where affluence and social status intersect. Exclusive neighborhoods like Bel Air in Los Angeles or the Hamptons in New York are as much about lifestyle as they are about the actual homes. Living in these areas signifies that one belongs to a particular social class and has access to networks of similarly wealthy and influential people. It's a subtle but powerful way of signaling status, as these neighborhoods offer privacy, security, and the association with a community of the ultra-wealthy.

Memberships and clubs have also become key ways for the wealthy to reinforce their social and cultural status. The Soho House, for instance, is an exclusive members-only club with locations in major cities worldwide. Membership is carefully curated to include artists, creatives, and industry leaders, and entry into the Soho House community isn't just about wealth—it's about fitting into a cultural narrative. Being a part of Soho House signifies a connection to a creative, progressive lifestyle, and it provides members with access to events, networking opportunities, and a sense of belonging among like-minded individuals.

Philanthropy and social causes are also increasingly part of how modern affluent individuals express their status. Supporting charitable causes, funding foundations, or even creating initiatives around social issues have become powerful ways for the wealthy to demonstrate influence and commitment to making a difference. Celebrities and business leaders often use their platforms and resources to champion causes like education, environmental conservation, and global health. For example, the Bill and Melinda Gates Foundation has become synonymous with global philanthropy, signaling not only wealth but a dedication to improving society. For the affluent, philanthropy is another way to reinforce social status while contributing to causes that align with their values.

In the end, luxury has come full circle as a social symbol. Despite the shift toward personal values and experiences, luxury still holds sway as a badge of belonging and a visible marker of success. It shapes social hierarchies, influences tastes, and sets aspirations, particularly within elite circles. The brands, experiences, and causes embraced by the affluent continue to set them apart, creating a distinct and exclusive culture around modern luxury.

## Concluding thoughts:

In today's world, luxury is about more than just wealth; it's a complex and evolving form of expression. From using their spending to reflect personal values, to seeking memorable experiences over material items, to reinforcing social status, the affluent are reshaping what luxury means in contemporary culture. For them, luxury has become a means of story-telling—an opportunity to project their identity, values, and place in the world. As a social and cultural symbol, luxury continues to shape tastes, define status, and reflect a deeply personal approach to what it means to live well.

# Media, Social Status, and the Reinvention of Wealth

Wealth and the pursuit of it are hardly new themes in human culture. For centuries, people have been drawn to the idea of luxury, success, and the prestige that comes with wealth. But today, in the digital age, this fascination has reached new heights. Thanks to the media—whether glossy magazines, reality TV, or the endless scroll of social media—images of wealth and affluence are everywhere, shaping our ideas of success and even reframing what it means to "make it" in life. Wealth, once considered a private achievement or family legacy, is now a public performance, broadcasted across platforms for the world to see.

This chapter dives into how media—traditional, digital, and social—has reshaped our understanding of wealth, making it not just a matter of financial status but an identity, a lifestyle, and even a brand. When we think of "rich," we're no longer just picturing bank accounts and assets. We're envisioning private jets, art collections, luxury getaways, and curated wardrobes. This shift in perception is largely a result of how media has created a kind of stage for wealth, with affluent lifestyles displayed in high definition for a global audience. From celebrities flaunting luxury vacations to influencers sharing their designer-filled lives, the media has made wealth more than an economic state—it's a visual and cultural currency.

For one, the portrayal of wealth in traditional media has changed significantly. Think back to the magazines of the 80s and 90s, with their iconic shots of celebrities in mansions or lavish spreads of private jets and beach vacations. These images gave the public a glimpse of lives beyond ordinary reach, but they were occasional and somewhat inaccessible. Today, those same images are no longer limited to magazine pages. They're on our phones, updated in real-time, with behind-the-scenes glimpses into the daily lives of the wealthy and powerful. We're no longer waiting for the next issue of Vogueto see wealth; instead, we're inundated with it daily, reshaping our ideas of affluence and accessibility.

Social media, particularly platforms like Instagram, TikTok, and YouTube, has played a huge role in democratizing the spectacle of wealth. Now anyone can create an aspirational lifestyle, carefully curating content that mirrors the aesthetics of the affluent. Influencers can build entire careers based on portraying a "luxurious" life, filled with travel, fashion, and gourmet dining—even if, behind the scenes, they're funded by brand partnerships or sponsorships. Social media has given rise to a form of "performative wealth," where it's less about actual wealth and more about the appearance of it. This performative aspect has created new standards for what it means to be wealthy, making luxury a matter of image, reputation, and digital footprint.

But there's another layer to this: the influence of media on how we aspire to wealth. The constant exposure to images of affluence has reshaped the aspirations of an entire generation. For many, success is no longer defined by a stable career or homeownership—it's about achieving a lifestyle that's visibly and publicly affluent. People are not only striving for financial success but also for social status and a life that can be displayed, shared, and celebrated. It's a form of "aspirationalism" fueled by digital media, where the goal isn't just to earn wealth but to embody and showcase it.

This chapter will explore how media has amplified the visibility of wealth and influenced consumer behavior. People want to live the lives they see online, and this desire has led to trends in consumption that are not only about owning luxury but about creating a curated, enviable existence. Brands have caught on, tailoring their messaging to reflect a new kind of aspirational consumer who isn't just buying products but adopting a lifestyle, aligning with values like exclusivity, sustainability, and uniqueness.

Ultimately, we'll see how the media's portrayal of wealth has not just fueled fascination but helped reinvent wealth itself. Today, being "wealthy" means more than just having money; it means having the visibility, the followers, the status, and the influence to project a life that others aspire to emulate. Wealth has become a public performance, a curated collection of moments meant to be seen and admired by others. In this sense, media doesn't just display wealth—it creates and sustains the modern image of what it means to be successful, setting the standards for the lives that we, consciously or unconsciously, aspire to lead.

So, let's dive in and explore how media has become a powerful tool in the reinvention of wealth, reshaping our dreams, our definitions of success, and, ultimately, our society's view on what it means to truly "live well."

# Chapter 4.1: The Power of Media in Shaping Wealth Narratives

Media has an extraordinary influence on how we understand and aspire to wealth. From the early days of film and print to the social media-driven culture of today, media has not only showcased wealth but shaped our perceptions of what it means to be wealthy. Through decades of evolving narratives, we've seen wealth portrayed as an inheritance of the elite, a reward for talent, and a symbol of social power. This chapter will dive into how these portrayals have changed over time and how each era's unique narrative of wealth continues to impact our collective view of success and aspiration.

## Historical Context: Wealth as Seen Through the Lens of Early Media

Media's fascination with wealth is not a recent phenomenon. From the early 20th century onward, traditional media forms like film, literature, and print magazines created images of wealth that set the tone for our understanding of success and status. These portrayals were often aspirational, reflecting the lives of the ultra-wealthy in ways that both dazzled and mystified the public.

One of the most iconic representations of wealth in early media is F. Scott Fitzgerald's The Great Gatsby, published in 1925. The novel paints a vivid picture of Jazz Age excess, with grand parties, opulent mansions, and characters who exude wealth and sophistication. Gatsby's mansion is not just a home; it's a symbol of ambition and desire, a palace built to win over the love of his life and impress high society. The imagery in Gatsby—the lavish parties, silk shirts, and champagne towers—served to portray wealth as something grand, desirable, and slightly elusive. The story wasn't just about money but about the lengths people would go to achieve social status and recognition. Gatsby himself became an enduring symbol of the American Dream and the idea that wealth could elevate a person to extraordinary heights, even if it couldn't necessarily guarantee happiness.

In Hollywood, Gone with the Wind (1939) continued to glamorize a life of wealth and opulence. Scarlett O'Hara, the film's headstrong heroine, lives in a grand plantation mansion, representing the "old money" of the American South. Scenes of sweeping staircases, elaborate gowns, and luxurious estates painted wealth as a kind of timeless inheritance, something associated with heritage and aristocracy. This type of wealth felt unattainable to most people, but it also fed a fascination with high society, old money, and the enduring idea that wealth was deeply linked to lineage and tradition.

In the 1950s and 60s, Life Magazine and Vanity Fair offered readers rare glimpses into the lives of America's wealthiest families, from the Rockefellers to the Vanderbilts. Through carefully staged photographs and in-depth features, these magazines invited readers to marvel at the lifestyles of the rich and famous. Life's coverage of Jackie Kennedy's tour of the White House in 1962, was a defining moment, showcasing wealth as dignified, elegant, and culturally influential. With her impeccable style and poise, Jackie became an icon of "old money" sophistication, representing a type of wealth that wasn't just about spending but about taste, class, and refined aesthetics.

These early portrayals laid the foundation for the "old money" aesthetic we recognize today: wealth that feels timeless, graceful, and understated. But as media evolved, so too did the narrative around wealth, moving from depictions of inherited privilege to stories of earned fortune and self-made success.

## The Rise of Celebrity Culture: Wealth as the New American Dream

By the latter half of the 20th century, a cultural shift was underway. Television was booming, the entertainment industry was expanding, and a new class of media stars was emerging. Unlike the "old money" elite who were often born into wealth, these figures were self-made celebrities—actors, musicians, and athletes who rose to fame through talent, hard work, and a bit of luck. Their stories offered a different version of the American Dream, one where anyone could achieve wealth, no matter their background.

One of the most influential figures in this era of media-driven wealth narratives was Oprah Winfrey. Rising from a difficult childhood marked by poverty and adversity, Oprah transformed herself into a media powerhouse. By the 1980s, her talk show, The Oprah Winfrey Show, had become a cultural phenomenon, and Oprah herself was one of the wealthiest women in America. But what made Oprah's story resonate so deeply was her relatability and vulnerability; she openly shared her struggles and successes, allowing the public to connect with her as a real person rather than an untouchable celebrity. Oprah became a symbol of self-made wealth, embodying the idea that hard work, resilience, and personal authenticity could lead to enormous success.

Then there was Michael Jordan, whose journey from a high school athlete to a global icon changed the game—literally. Jordan's success on the basketball court, combined with his lucrative endorsement deals with brands like Nike, turned him into a sports and business mogul. He was more than an athlete; he was a brand, and his story was that of a young man who had parlayed his talents into a fortune. For fans around the world, Jordan represented the idea that wealth could be the reward for excellence and determination. His iconic partnership with Nike even created the Air Jordan brand, establishing a new model for how athletes could transcend sports to build personal empires.

In the music world, Beyoncé and Jay-Z have become symbols of self-made wealth. From humble beginnings, both artists rose to the top of the music industry, and together they've built an empire that spans entertainment, fashion, and lifestyle. Beyoncé and Jay-Z's wealth isn't just about the music they create; it's about the powerful brand they've established. They're seen not only as entertainers but as influential cultural figures who have shaped music, fashion, and even social causes. Beyoncé's commitment to issues like women's empowerment and Black culture has added depth to her brand, making her wealth a reflection of her values and beliefs.

The rise of self-made celebrity wealth has been amplified by media coverage that focuses not just on what these figures earn but on how they live, what they wear, and how they spend their time. MTV Cribs in the early 2000s took television viewers on tours of celebrity homes, showcasing their extravagant lifestyles and luxurious possessions. These programs gave fans a peek behind the curtain, allowing them to see the mansions, cars, and designer clothes that came with celebrity wealth. Suddenly, the public was exposed to wealth on a personal level, with celebrities willingly opening their doors to showcase their success.

This portrayal of wealth as accessible and achievable had a profound effect on popular culture. While the old money families of the early 20th century felt distant and unattainable, the celebrities of the late 20th century felt like they were "of the people." Fans could identify with them, aspire to their success, and imagine themselves in similar positions. The American Dream was redefined—not as something tied to family legacy or aristocratic lineage, but as something anyone could attain through talent, hard work, and branding.

This shift in media-driven wealth narratives gave rise to a new archetype: the self-made mogul. Figures like Richard Branson, who built the Virgin brand from scratch, and Elon Musk, who rose to prominence with Tesla and SpaceX, embody this archetype. These individuals are celebrated not only for their wealth but for their innovation, risk-taking, and ability to disrupt industries. They represent the idea that wealth can be created, not just inherited, and that success can come from challenging the status quo.

## The Evolution of Wealth Narratives in Modern Media

Today, media continues to shape wealth narratives, but the landscape has become even more complex with the advent of social media, streaming services, and online content platforms. We're no longer limited to the lives of actors, athletes, or corporate moguls. Now, influencers, entrepreneurs, and even digital content creators can become symbols of wealth, reshaping how we perceive success and status.

Social media has democratized the portrayal of wealth, allowing anyone with a following and a smartphone to create an aspirational lifestyle. Instagram and TikTok are filled with images of exotic vacations, luxury fashion hauls, and high-end dining experiences. These portrayals are carefully curated to project an image of wealth, even if, in some cases, it's more about appearance than reality. For many followers, these influencers represent a new kind of wealth narrative, one where success is about visibility, popularity, and lifestyle.

In the digital age, influencer Kylie Jenner has taken the wealth narrative to new levels. When Jenner was declared the youngest self-made billionaire by Forbes in 2019, it stirred controversy and debate. But the title reflected the modern reality: Kylie had built a beauty empire through social media, leveraging her platform to launch and promote her brand, Kylie Cosmetics. Her story is emblematic of how the media-driven narrative of wealth has evolved to include not only traditional success but digital influence.

Netflix has also contributed to the fascination with wealth through popular shows such as Selling Sunset and Bling Empire, which showcase the lives of the ultra-wealthy in real estate and high society. These shows aren't just about wealth; they're about lifestyles, relationships, and the allure of luxury, presented in a way that feels personal and intimate. Viewers don't just see the wealth; they get a behind-the-scenes look at the drama, decisions, and personal struggles of the rich, making them feel closer to that world than ever before.

This accessibility has created a new form of aspirationalism, where viewers are not only interested in the symbols of wealth but in the lives and personalities of the wealthy. Media has transformed wealth from a distant concept to something that feels achievable, or at the very least, relatable. We no longer just see wealth in terms of dollar amounts or material possessions. Wealth is now a brand, a lifestyle, and an identity, carefully curated and shared across multiple platforms.

From early 20th-century literature and film to the rise of self-made celebrities and the influence of social media, media has played a powerful role in shaping how we view wealth. Each era's portrayal of wealth reflects the values, aspirations, and dreams of its time, creating a narrative that has grown more accessible, personal, and aspirational with each passing decade. In today's world, wealth is as much about image and influence as it is about money, and media continues to be the lens through which we interpret, aspire to, and redefine what it means to be truly successful.

## Chapter 4.2: The Digital Revolution: Social Media as a Wealth Showcase

In the past, glimpses of wealth were confined to glossy magazine covers, movies, or the rare paparazzi photo that made the front page. But with the rise of social media, the display of wealth has become more visible, more accessible, and more aspirational than ever before. Instagram, YouTube, and TikTok have transformed how we experience luxury, putting wealth on display in a way that feels immediate and personal. Today, anyone with a smartphone can scroll through feeds filled with designer clothes, private jets, and luxury homes, creating a daily, visual culture of opulence that has changed how we think about wealth.

This chapter explores how Instagram has become the main stage for wealth showcase, how the influencer economy has created new standards of success and aspiration, and how aspirational content on social media has turned self-made entrepreneurs into symbols of modern achievement.

## Instagram: The Digital Billboard of Luxury

Instagram has emerged as the ultimate platform for displaying wealth in the modern era. Unlike Facebook or Twitter, Instagram is visual-first, making it the perfect medium for showcasing the aesthetics of luxury. With its high-quality images, carefully curated feeds, and aspirational content, Instagram is essentially a digital billboard where influencers, celebrities, and brands can share a highly polished version of their lifestyles with the world.

For example, take Kim Kardashian. With her massive following, Kim has turned her Instagram feed into a digital showcase of her wealth and lifestyle. Her posts include everything from snapshots of her designer wardrobe and private jet flights to her luxurious vacations and high-end skincare line. Each post is a carefully crafted piece of aspirational content, painting a picture of a life filled with luxury and exclusivity. Her followers see these posts not just as moments in her life but as symbols of success. To many, Kim isn't just a reality TV star; she's an icon of modern wealth and style.

Then there's Jay Shetty, a former monk turned motivational speaker who has built an influential personal brand on Instagram. With over 14 million followers, Shetty uses the platform to share insights on mindfulness, relationships, and personal growth. His engaging posts include short inspirational videos, thought-provoking quotes, and behind-the-scenes glimpses of his work. Shetty's approach isn't just about projecting success but fostering a sense of community and empowerment among his followers. By blending authenticity with practical wisdom, he has positioned himself as a relatable figure in the self-help space, using Instagram as a powerful tool to amplify his message and reach millions worldwide.

Instagram has become a digital playground for wealth, and it's not just celebrities or moguls who are in on it. Influencers across a range of industries have also transformed their Instagram feeds into carefully curated showcases of aspirational lifestyles. For instance, travel influencers share shots of exotic destinations, luxury hotel stays, and first-class flights, creating a narrative that travel itself is a luxury lifestyle choice. Fashion influencers flaunt designer pieces, often gifted by brands, in aesthetically coordinated posts that exude glamour and sophistication.

The aspirational quality of these posts is irresistible to followers. For many, scrolling through Instagram is like flipping through a digital magazine of modern luxury, where each post is an idealized version of success. It's a platform where wealth isn't just displayed; it's celebrated, envied, and, ultimately, desired. And for those who post, Instagram has become a way to shape and project a personal brand built on status and exclusivity.

## Influencer Economy: From Social Media Stars to Wealth Icons

The rise of social media has also changed the dynamics of wealth itself, giving birth to the influencer economy. While celebrities once reigned as the primary symbols of wealth and success, influencers have redefined what it means to be a modern-day icon. Today, many influencers have massive followings, which they leverage to build lucrative partnerships, command high fees for brand collaborations, and, in some cases, even launch their own product lines. These influencers have turned their personal lifestyles into highly profitable businesses, transforming social media presence into real-world wealth.

Take Chiara Ferragni, one of the earliest and most successful fashion influencers. Ferragni started as a fashion blogger, but her keen sense of style and ability to connect with her audience helped her amass millions of followers. Over time, she became a global influencer and launched her own fashion line, The Chiara Ferragni Collection. Her brand is now valued at millions, and she is often seen rubbing shoulders with top designers and celebrities. Ferragni's journey illustrates the power of the influencer economy; she turned her personal brand into an empire, becoming not only a social media star but also a wealthy businesswoman.

The influencer economy has also shifted the dynamics of celebrity itself. Unlike traditional celebrities who rose to fame through music, film, or sports, many influencers gain their following simply by sharing their lives, tastes, and personalities online. James Charles, a beauty influencer, is a prime example. By sharing makeup tutorials, product reviews, and personal stories, Charles built a massive following on YouTube and Instagram. His influence caught the attention of major beauty brands, leading to collaborations, sponsorships, and eventually his own line of beauty products. Charles' wealth and success are the direct result of his online presence, illustrating how social media can be a gateway to modern wealth.

Another notable example is Ramit Sethi, the finance expert and author of *I Will Teach You to Be Rich*. Sethi started by sharing practical financial advice on his blog, and his expertise quickly gained him a loyal following on Instagram. He leverages his popularity to promote his courses and resources, empowering followers to master their finances, negotiate salaries, and invest confidently. Sethi's story highlights a key aspect of the influencer economy: he uses his platform not just to share tips but to create a thriving business that helps others achieve financial freedom. For his followers, Sethi is more than an influencer; he's a trusted guide showing how social media can be a powerful tool for building wealth and financial literacy.

Let's also consider Ryan Serhant, a prominent real estate broker and media personality. Serhant began his career in real estate in 2008 and quickly rose to prominence, leveraging his expertise to build a substantial following on Instagram. He utilizes the platform to showcase luxury property listings, share market insights, and provide behind-the-scenes glimpses into his professional life. Serhant's strategic use of social media has not only enhanced his personal brand but also contributed to the success of his brokerage firm, SERHANT., which emphasizes innovative marketing and media production. His journey underscores how effectively leveraging social media can transform a traditional career into a dynamic personal brand, offering valuable lessons for professionals across industries.

In many ways, influencers have become the new wealth icons. They represent a kind of success that feels accessible yet aspirational, creating a bridge between traditional celebrity and everyday life. Through strategic brand collaborations, product placements, and personal branding, influencers have redefined wealth as something that can be achieved through digital platforms. This shift has made wealth feel more achievable, giving millions of followers the sense that they, too, could achieve success if they build the right following and cultivate the right brand.

## Aspirational Content: Social Media as a Platform for Self-Made Success

One of the most transformative aspects of social media is its ability to showcase self-made success. Instagram, YouTube, and TikTok have become spaces where self-made entrepreneurs, beauty gurus, real estate experts, consultants and even young tech founders can document their journeys to financial success. This new kind of aspirational content has reshaped how we view wealth, offering a narrative that is less about privilege and more about personal achievement and hard work.

For example, Gary Vaynerchuk, a digital marketing entrepreneur who uses his social media channels to share his journey, offer advice, and inspire others to pursue their entrepreneurial dreams. Vaynerchuk's content often includes clips from speaking engagements, interviews, and behind-the-scenes moments from his daily life. His approach to wealth is relatable and down-to-earth; he doesn't flaunt luxury possessions, but he openly shares his strategies for success, making his content feel both motivational and practical. For his followers, Vaynerchuk represents a model of self-made success that feels achievable. He's proof that wealth isn't just about status—it's about the hustle, the grind, and the relentless pursuit of goals.

Similarly, luxury real estate moguls like Fredrik Eklund and Josh Altman have leveraged social media to build thriving empires. Fredrik Eklund, a star of *Million Dollar Listing New York*, started as a real estate broker with a flair for connecting with high-net-worth clients. Through Instagram, Eklund showcases multimillion-dollar properties, shares market insights, and offers glimpses into his jet-setting lifestyle. His posts are a blend of aspiration and authenticity, resonating with both potential clients and fans. Eklund's success story exemplifies how social media can serve as a powerful platform for self-made wealth, transforming expertise in real estate into a globally recognized luxury brand.

This shift is also evident on YouTube and TikTok, where young entrepreneurs share their journeys in real-time, documenting everything from the challenges of starting a business to the excitement of closing a big deal. Emma Chamberlain, a YouTuber and influencer known for her unique, relatable style, has captivated millions of followers with her candid approach to content. Her success led to brand collaborations, a popular podcast, and even her own coffee line, Chamberlain Coffee. For fans, Chamberlain's journey from an ordinary teenager to a business-savvy influencer embodies the new model of success in the digital age.

What makes these self-made success stories so impactful is the transparency and authenticity with which they're shared. Unlike traditional portrayals of wealth, which often feel distant or unattainable, these influencers allow followers to witness the journey from start to finish. They share not just the glamorous moments but the hard work, late nights, and personal sacrifices that go into building a brand. This type of aspirational content feels genuine and inspiring, reinforcing the idea that wealth can be created from the ground up.

As we continue to navigate the digital age, social media will undoubtedly play an even greater role in shaping our views on wealth and success. It has already blurred the lines between traditional wealth and digital influence, creating a new paradigm where wealth is both a personal journey and a public performance. The digital revolution has transformed wealth into a cultural currency, where success isn't just achieved—it's shared, celebrated, and made visible for all to see.

# Chapter 4.3: Luxury and Consumerism in the Spotlight

In our digital world, luxury has taken on new life, amplified by the visibility and reach of social media. Instagram, Facebook, and TikTok have transformed how we perceive and consume luxury, making high-end brands more visible and aspirational than ever before. What was once the private domain of the wealthy is now openly displayed, making luxury both an attainable dream and a status symbol that everyone wants a piece of. With influencers, brand partnerships, and a constant stream of luxury content in the spotlight, consumerism has been redefined, placing luxury brands front and center in a way that feels accessible yet exclusive.

In this chapter, we'll explore how social media has transformed luxury into a widely visible status symbol, how FOMO (the Fear of Missing Out) drives consumer behavior, and the role of brand partnerships and sponsorships in building a powerful, aspirational connection to wealth.

## Luxury as a Status Symbol in the Social Media Era

Social media has turned luxury into a status symbol in a way that feels both personal and public. High-end brands Louis Vuitton, Gucci, and Chanel have mastered the art of using platforms like Instagram to reach consumers directly, posting glamorous images of their latest products, which are often worn or displayed by celebrities, influencers, and high-profile individuals. In doing so, these brands have created a new level of visibility and exclusivity; their products are not only known but are desired by millions of people around the world. Today, seeing a Louis Vuitton handbag or a Gucci belt on Instagram isn't rare; it's part of the daily visual culture of social media.

This level of visibility has had a profound impact on how we view luxury goods. In the past, luxury items were more private and exclusive, something only seen on the wealthy or in the pages of fashion magazines. Now, anyone can scroll through their feed and see influencers and celebrities showing off their latest designer purchases, creating a visual narrative that says, "This is what success looks like." For instance, seeing celebrities like Kylie Jenner pose with her collection of designer handbags and luxury cars reinforces the idea that these items are symbols of wealth and status. It's not just about the product; it's about what the product represents—a life of glamour, success, and exclusivity.

Take the Hermès Birkin bag, which has always been a luxury symbol due to its high price and exclusivity. In the social media era, owning a Birkin has become a status badge for influencers and celebrities alike. When influencers Jeffree Star or Kim Kardashian show off their Birkin collections, it's more than just a casual post; it's a statement of wealth, exclusivity, and fashion influence. Followers see these bags not only as beautiful items but as representations of a lifestyle they aspire to achieve. The visibility of these luxury goods on social media has made them more desirable than ever before, elevating them from mere possessions to icons of success.

This dynamic has also led to the rise of more affordable luxury items, as brands recognize that not everyone can afford a Birkin but might still want to buy into the Hermès brand. For example, smaller items like Hermès scarves or Gucci belts have become immensely popular because they allow consumers to own a piece of the luxury pie without the enormous price tag. These items are still expensive, but they're much more attainable than the top-tier products, making them perfect for a market that craves luxury but may not have the budget to fully dive into it. This "entry-level luxury" approach lets a broader audience experience a taste of the luxury lifestyle, reinforcing the brand's status while widening its reach.

Through social media, luxury goods have transcended their role as symbols of wealth reserved for an elite few; they have become objects of desire that feel almost within reach for a global audience. The constant stream of images featuring these items has created a culture where luxury is no longer something private or exclusive but something visible, shared, and aspirational. And while these items remain out of reach for many, their online presence makes them feel tantalizingly close.

## FOMO: The Fear of Missing Out and the Power of Social Comparison

The Fear of Missing Out, or FOMO, is one of the most powerful drivers of consumer behavior in the social media era. We've all felt it—that nagging feeling that others are living more exciting, successful, or glamorous lives. On social media, luxury products and experiences are frequently on display, creating a digital world where wealth and status are not only visible but actively celebrated. Seeing influencers on private jets, celebrities vacationing in the Maldives, or friends posting photos of their new designer shoes can make us feel like we're missing out, even if those lifestyles were never within our reach to begin with.

FOMO is especially prevalent on Instagram, where the platform's visual nature and curated feeds intensify feelings of social comparison. When someone sees influencers jetting off to exotic destinations, staying in high-end hotels, or enjoying designer shopping sprees, it's easy to feel like they should be doing the same. The curated feeds of influencers and celebrities often portray a life that feels perfect and carefree, making followers feel that they, too, should be living a similar lifestyle. It's this sense of "keeping up" that has contributed to a culture where luxury consumption is not only desirable but feels almost necessary to fit into the digital social scene.

One example of how FOMO drives consumer behavior is the phenomenon of "it" bags, shoes, or accessories that trend on social media. When a product like the Gucci Marmont bag or the Balenciaga Triple S sneakers starts gaining popularity on Instagram, it quickly becomes a must-have item for fashion-conscious consumers. The desire to own these items isn't always based on personal taste; often, it's driven by the fear of being left out of a trend that seems to define what's "in" at the moment. Social media has created an environment where certain luxury items become symbols of social currency, giving people a way to signal their awareness of current trends and their ability to participate in them.

For some, this FOMO-driven consumerism leads to what is known as "aspirational spending"—buying items that may be financially out of reach simply to project a certain lifestyle. Even if someone has to save up for months or go into debt to buy a designer handbag, the payoff is the feeling of being part of the luxury culture they see online. This behavior has become so common that brands have started capitalizing on it by creating "drop" models, where limited-edition items are released in small quantities to create exclusivity and heighten FOMO. Brands like Supreme, Louis Vuitton, and Nike have all used this model, selling out of products within minutes of release and creating a buzz that makes followers feel they're missing out if they don't get in on the latest trend.

Social media's power to create FOMO has intensified consumer culture, making luxury items feel both accessible and unattainable at the same time. Even if these products are out of financial reach for many, the constant exposure to them on social media makes people feel as though they should be able to own them. This tension between desire and inaccessibility fuels an endless cycle of consumerism, where followers continually look to luxury as a way to fulfill their own social aspirations.

## Brand Partnerships and Sponsorships: Influencers as Luxury Ambassadors

One of the most influential aspects of social media's relationship with luxury is the rise of brand partnerships and sponsorships. In the age of Instagram, influencers are not just posting their luxurious lives; they're actively partnering with luxury brands to promote aspirational products. Whether it's a sponsored post showing off a $10,000 handbag or an invitation to a luxury fashion show, these partnerships reinforce the connection between wealth, personal branding, and consumerism.

For example, influencers Aimee Song and Camila Coelho have become ambassadors for major luxury brands, regularly posting about their collaborations with brands including Chanel, Dior, and Louis Vuitton. These partnerships are mutually beneficial: luxury brands gain access to the influencers' audiences, while influencers gain credibility and the opportunity to align themselves with prestigious brands. When Aimee Song posts about attending a Dior fashion show, for instance, it's more than just a post; it's a signal to her followers that she's reached a level of influence and status that gives her access to one of the most exclusive events in fashion. This kind of content has a powerful aspirational pull, creating a desire among followers to attain not just luxury products but the status that comes with them.

Sponsored content, especially with luxury brands, has also led to the rise of "luxury giveaways," where influencers host contests to win high-end items like designer bags or luxury skincare products. These giveaways create a sense of excitement and exclusivity, with followers eagerly participating for a chance to own items they might not be able to afford on their own. For brands, this approach expands their reach to a broader audience while keeping the aura of luxury intact. The influencer doesn't just promote a product; they promote an experience of luxury, one that followers aspire to have for themselves.

Another example is the phenomenon of "luxury unboxings," where influencers film themselves opening high-end purchases, from designer bags to luxury cars. The unboxing process itself becomes a performance, where influencers walk their followers through every detail of the product, sharing the excitement and exclusivity of owning a luxury item. For viewers, these unboxings create a vicarious thrill, allowing them to experience a taste of luxury, even if only from behind a screen. This type of content blurs the line between advertising and entertainment, transforming luxury consumerism into a form of aspirational storytelling.

The aspirational quality of these brand partnerships has a powerful impact on social media culture. Followers are not just watching influencers promote luxury products; they're engaging with a narrative of success, style, and status. The visibility of these luxury goods on social media creates an aspirational loop, where followers not only want to achieve financial success but also to display it in the most visible way possible. Luxury is no longer just a private indulgence; it's a badge of achievement and a symbol of social standing that is meant to be displayed, shared, and admired.

## Chapter 4.4: The New Age of Financial Influencers

In recent years, the concept of wealth and financial success has taken on new meanings in the digital world. Social media has given rise to a wave of financial influencers—figures who use platforms like Instagram, YouTube, TikTok, and Twitter to share their insights on building wealth, managing money, and creating financial independence. This group, often referred to as "finfluencers," has transformed financial advice from something formal and institutional into an accessible, lifestyle-focused conversation. People are not only learning about money management and investing from these influencers; they're also watching them live out their financial philosophies, often showcasing their own wealth as evidence that their strategies work.

This chapter explores the role of financial influencers in shaping modern perspectives on wealth, the blend of personal finance with lifestyle branding, and the ways in which social media has democratized financial advice, making it more accessible to people of all backgrounds. We'll also look at the challenges and risks that come with relying on influencers for financial guidance in an environment where not all advice is created equal.

## Personal Finance as Lifestyle: Financial Influencers as Wealth Icons

In traditional media, finance and wealth were often discussed in professional, almost academic terms. Financial advice came from bank advisors, financial planners, or columnists in major publications. But social media has shifted this narrative, making financial advice feel personal, accessible, and even aspirational. Influencers including Dave Ramsey, Robert Kiyosaki, and Grant Cardone have pioneered a new form of financial advice that blends practical guidance with personal branding, transforming finance from a dry topic into a lifestyle.

Take Dave Ramsey, for example. Known for his "baby steps" approach to personal finance, Ramsey has built an empire around teaching people how to get out of debt, save money, and invest for the future. He doesn't just offer advice—he offers a roadmap for financial freedom. Ramsey's personality and firm approach resonate with his followers, who view him as a mentor. He hosts radio shows, publishes best-selling books, and shares his financial philosophies on social media, reinforcing the idea that financial success is attainable if you're disciplined and stick to his principles. Ramsey's own financial success serves as proof of his method, giving followers a tangible example of what's possible if they adopt his practices.

Similarly, Robert Kiyosaki, author of Rich Dad Poor Dad, has become a prominent voice in personal finance by emphasizing the importance of investing, financial education, and building assets rather than relying on traditional employment. Kiyosaki's philosophy is largely about challenging conventional views on wealth-building, encouraging people to pursue financial freedom by acquiring assets like real estate and investments rather than focusing solely on a high-paying job. He uses social media to reinforce his teachings, sharing stories about his own investments and success, positioning himself not just as a teacher but as someone who embodies the financial independence he advocates for.

Grant Cardone, a self-made millionaire known for his high-energy approach to wealth-building, takes a different route. Cardone's philosophy is based on a mindset of abundance and aggression—he encourages his followers to think big, take risks, and scale their efforts. His signature 10X rule, which promotes amplifying one's goals and efforts by ten times, has gained a massive following. Cardone's social media presence is filled with posts about his ventures in real estate, his private jet, and his luxurious lifestyle. By showcasing his wealth as proof of his financial principles, he creates an aspirational brand around financial success. Cardone's followers aren't just learning about real estate; they're buying into a mindset of ambition and boldness.

These financial influencers blend financial education with a branded lifestyle that makes wealth-building look exciting, achievable, and desirable. Their followers are not just learning how to manage money—they're watching these influencers live out their philosophies. By positioning themselves as both teachers and living examples, they create a strong connection with their audience, showing that financial success isn't just about knowledge; it's also about how you live and present yourself.

## Financial Aspiration and Accessibility: The Rise of Everyday Finfluencers

Social media platforms like TikTok, Instagram, and YouTube have democratized financial advice, allowing people from all walks of life to share their experiences and insights on money management. This shift has led to the rise of "everyday" financial influencers who may not be millionaires but who offer relatable and practical advice on budgeting, saving, investing, and building wealth. These finfluencers make financial success feel accessible to a broad audience, creating a new model of wealth-building that feels both relatable and achievable.

On TikTok, for example, short-form videos have become a popular way to share quick financial tips. Influencers Humphrey Yang and Erika Kullberg create content that ranges from breaking down stock market basics to explaining credit card hacks. Their videos are concise, engaging, and often have a friendly, conversational tone that makes complex financial topics easy to understand. Yang, for instance, has gained popularity for his "Money Tips" series, where he explains financial concepts in a way that feels relevant and accessible to younger audiences. He covers topics including investing in index funds, paying off student loans, and building an emergency fund—all in under a minute.

Then there's Erika Kullberg, a former lawyer turned financial influencer, who specializes in sharing financial hacks, often related to credit cards and saving money. Her TikTok videos, which show her sharing tricks for getting refunds on flights, disputing fees, or maximizing credit card rewards, have resonated with viewers who want practical advice they can use immediately. Kullberg's approach is highly relatable; she's not showing off wealth but rather empowering her followers with tips to stretch their dollars and get more value from everyday spending.

Instagram and YouTube have also become home to a new wave of finance content creators who share their personal journeys to financial independence. Influencers Graham Stephan and Andrei Jikh have built large followings on YouTube by documenting their experiences with investing, real estate, and personal finance. Graham Stephan, for example, shares his story of building wealth through real estate investment, offering practical insights into how he saved, invested, and eventually became financially independent. His videos are filled with step-by-step breakdowns, from buying rental properties to managing tenants, giving viewers a window into his journey while teaching them how to apply similar principles.

Andrei Jikh, known for his videos on investing and the stock market, takes a more technical approach. With a background in magic, he uses creative visuals and storytelling to explain compound interest, stock options, and cryptocurrency. His transparency about his own investments and his occasional losses makes him relatable to viewers who appreciate his honesty. For many, Jikh's success isn't just inspiring—it's informative, making them feel that wealth-building is within reach if they're willing to learn and take calculated risks.

These everyday financial influencers make wealth-building feel like an attainable journey rather than a distant dream. They provide a sense of financial accessibility that traditional media often lacks, giving their audiences a roadmap to achieve financial success, no matter their starting point.

## The Double-Edged Sword of Financial Influencing: Risks and Authenticity

While financial influencers have made personal finance more accessible, their popularity also brings certain risks. Not all financial advice on social media is reliable, and the line between genuine financial guidance and self-promotion can sometimes blur. Some influencers may prioritize engagement and views over responsible advice, leading followers to take financial risks without fully understanding the consequences. This shift in how financial advice is consumed raises important questions about the authenticity and reliability of the information being shared.

One risk is that some financial influencers may oversimplify complex topics or make investment strategies sound easier than they are. For example, during the 2020 and 2021 surge in cryptocurrency interest, numerous TikTok influencers promoted Bitcoin, Ethereum, and even lesser-known "altcoins" as surefire paths to wealth. Some of these influencers encouraged viewers to "get rich quick" by investing in volatile assets without fully explaining the risks involved. For young investors or those new to finance, this kind of advice can be misleading, creating unrealistic expectations and, in some cases, leading to significant financial losses.

Authenticity is another key factor. While some influencers share transparent, practical advice, others may present a highly polished version of their lives that doesn't fully reflect the reality of their financial situations. For instance, an influencer might display a luxury lifestyle funded by brand partnerships, sponsorships, or even debt, while portraying it as a result of savvy investing. This creates a distorted picture of financial success, leading followers to believe that wealth is easier to achieve than it truly is.

To combat these risks, some platforms have started requiring influencers to disclose sponsored content and partnerships, but financial advice remains largely unregulated on social media. This means that followers must approach financial influencers with a critical eye, researching strategies independently and considering the potential downsides before making financial decisions. The democratization of financial advice is powerful, but it also requires a level of discernment and skepticism from followers to ensure they're following reliable advice.

In this new age of financial influencers, personal finance has become not just a subject of discussion but a lifestyle and a brand. Influencers like Dave Ramsey, Robert Kiyosaki, and Grant Cardone have shown that financial advice can be empowering and even aspirational, creating brands around their unique approaches to wealth-building. Platforms like TikTok, YouTube, and Instagram have made financial advice accessible to everyday individuals, with influencers sharing practical tips, personal journeys, and strategies that feel relatable and attainable.

However, this shift toward financial advice on social media also comes with risks. The line between authentic advice and self-promotion can be thin, and not all advice is created equal. Followers must be cautious, doing their own research and approaching financial decisions thoughtfully to avoid potential pitfalls.

Ultimately, financial influencers have transformed the conversation around money, creating a more inclusive and democratized landscape where wealth-building feels possible for everyone. But as with all forms of influence, it's essential to remember that true financial success isn't just about what you see online—it's about making informed choices that align with your own goals and values. As the world of financial influencers continues to grow, so too does the responsibility for both influencers and their audiences to engage with financial advice that is both practical and sustainable.

## Chapter 4.5: The Role of Traditional Media: Magazines, Television, and Film

In the age of social media and online influencers, traditional media might seem a bit outdated. Yet, magazines, television, and film still hold significant influence over how we perceive wealth, power, and luxury. From high-profile magazines like Forbes and Vogue to the hit shows Billions, Succession, and The Crown, traditional media outlets continue to captivate audiences with portrayals of the ultra-wealthy. These portrayals don't just offer glimpses into luxurious lifestyles; they shape our understanding of wealth by mixing admiration with critique, sparking both envy and introspection in audiences around the world.

This chapter explores how traditional media reinforces societal views on wealth and status. We'll look at how television and film delve into the complexities of the lives of the rich, how celebrity news and financial journalism keep the public's fascination with the wealthy alive, and how magazines have built a legacy around luxury branding that defines what it means to live "the good life."

## Television and Film: Romanticizing and Humanizing the Ultra-Wealthy

Television shows and films have long been fascinated with wealth, power, and the complexities that come with both. In recent years, Billions, Succession, and The Crown have taken this fascination to new levels by diving into the messy, sometimes ruthless world of the ultra-wealthy. These shows don't just showcase glamorous lives; they also explore the personal struggles, moral dilemmas, and psychological conflicts that often accompany great wealth.

Take Billions, for instance. The show follows billionaire hedge fund manager Bobby Axelrod, whose wealth and power allow him to live an enviable life filled with luxury, high-stakes investments, and influence over politicians and social circles. But while Axelrod's life is a display of extreme wealth and power, the show also reveals the costs of his ambition. Axelrod is constantly navigating ethical gray areas, manipulating people, and facing pressure from rivals like U.S. Attorney Chuck Rhoades, who is intent on taking him down. This tension between wealth and morality gives the audience a nuanced view of Axelrod. While viewers may admire his success, they also witness the price he pays for it, blurring the line between admiration and critique.

Similarly, Succession is a brilliant exploration of the lives of the Roy family, a media empire dynasty whose wealth and power exceed most people's imagination. On the surface, the show is filled with lavish settings, from private jets and five-star resorts to custom-tailored wardrobes and penthouse suites. But at its core, Succession is a dark look at family dynamics twisted by immense wealth and ambition. Each member of the Roy family is flawed and ambitious, grappling with issues of loyalty, betrayal, and a desperate need for approval from their father, Logan Roy, the family's powerful patriarch. The show doesn't shy away from the uglier side of wealth—manipulation, rivalry, and a constant battle for power—making the Roy family's wealth seem as much a curse as it is a blessing.

Then there's The Crown, a series that dramatizes the life and reign of Queen Elizabeth II and the British royal family. While the series offers a sumptuous view of royal life, with its palaces, jewels, and state functions, it also presents the royal family as individuals burdened by duty, tradition, and often a lack of personal freedom. Episodes exploring Queen Elizabeth's personal sacrifices, Prince Charles's struggles with his public image, or Princess Diana's battles with the expectations placed upon her offer a more complex, humanized view of these famous figures. The Crown manages to both glamorize and critique the royal lifestyle, leaving viewers in awe of the wealth and power but also sympathetic to the constraints that come with such a life.

These shows all share a common thread: they portray the ultra-wealthy not as caricatures but as complex characters with struggles, flaws, and aspirations. The wealth displayed on screen is mesmerizing, but it also comes with strings attached, making the audience feel a mixture of envy and relief. In showing both the privileges and the pitfalls of extreme wealth, television and film shape our views of what it truly means to live as one of the elite, revealing that, in many ways, the price of wealth can be surprisingly high.

## Celebrity News and Financial Journalism: A Constant Fascination with Wealth

Traditional media has also fueled our fascination with wealth through celebrity news and financial journalism. Publications, websites, and shows dedicated to celebrity gossip and business news keep the public informed—and often enthralled—by the financial ups and downs of the rich and famous. This ongoing media coverage doesn't just inform; it helps frame the wealthy as figures of both admiration and scrutiny, adding to their allure while holding them accountable for their actions.

Celebrity news outlets People, TMZ, and Entertainment Tonight provide constant updates on the lives of actors, musicians, athletes, and reality stars. From high-profile divorces and lavish weddings to scandals and financial controversies, these outlets feed the public's desire to know every detail of celebrities' lives. For example, the media coverage of Kim Kardashian and Kanye West's split included details on their shared assets, real estate holdings, and luxury possessions. Such reports offer a glimpse into the financial realities of the ultra-wealthy, humanizing them while also reinforcing the notion that their lives are defined by extraordinary privilege.

Financial journalism has taken this fascination even further, focusing on the wealth of CEOs, entrepreneurs, and high-profile investors. Forbes, Bloomberg, and The Wall Street Journal provide in-depth reporting on the wealth of tech giants Elon Musk, Jeff Bezos, and Mark Zuckerberg, tracking their net worth and covering their business ventures. When Elon Musk overtook Jeff Bezos as the richest person in the world, the media frenzy around their "wealth race" captivated audiences, turning billionaires into modern-day celebrities. By framing Musk and Bezos as rivals, the media not only highlighted their immense wealth but also played into the public's fascination with the competition, power, and influence of the ultra-wealthy.

Even celebrity-driven financial journalism has become part of this landscape. CNBC's Secret Lives of the Super Rich provides a glimpse into the lives of the ultra-wealthy, featuring everything from multimillion-dollar homes and private islands to rare collectibles and luxury cars. Each episode feels like a mini-documentary on wealth, showcasing the possessions and lifestyles that only the richest individuals can afford. For viewers, it's a chance to live vicariously through the experiences of the elite, seeing the opulence, exclusivity, and indulgence that comes with extreme wealth.

Financial journalism also covers the darker side of wealth, exposing corporate scandals, insider trading, and unethical business practices. The downfall of Bernie Madoff and the bankruptcy of Enron, for example, were widely covered in the media, serving as cautionary tales about the dangers of unchecked ambition and greed. Stories like these remind the public that wealth can come at a cost and that not all wealthy individuals are worthy of admiration. This balance between glamorizing wealth and exposing its flaws keeps audiences captivated, reinforcing the complex relationship between society and the rich.

## Magazines and Luxury Branding: Setting Standards for Wealth and Lifestyle

Print magazines, despite the rise of digital media, remain powerful symbols of luxury and lifestyle, showcasing the latest trends in fashion, travel, and high-end living. Vogue, Forbes, and Robb Report have become synonymous with wealth and success, creating a standard for luxury that millions aspire to.

Vogue, one of the most iconic fashion magazines in the world, has long been associated with luxury, style, and exclusivity. The magazine's pages are filled with high-fashion editorials, designer interviews, and profiles of the world's most influential people, from celebrities to entrepreneurs. A Vogue cover featuring Rihanna in custom couture is more than just a fashion statement; it's a celebration of Rihanna's success and influence. Each issue of Vogue serves as a guide to the latest trends in luxury, from designer handbags and jewelry to the most exclusive travel destinations. By highlighting the lifestyles of the rich and fashionable, Vogue creates a world of aspiration, where readers are invited to imagine themselves living lives of beauty, sophistication, and style.

Forbes takes a different approach to luxury branding, focusing on wealth, business success, and entrepreneurship. Its Forbes Billionaires List and 30 Under 30—are benchmarks of success, identifying the wealthiest and most influential individuals across industries. The Forbes Billionaires List, serves as a ranking of the world's wealthiest people, turning billionaires into public figures who are admired, analyzed, and even scrutinized by readers. For entrepreneurs and professionals, making it onto a Forbes list is more than an honor; it's a symbol of having "made it" in the world of wealth and influence. Forbes' articles on wealth-building, investment strategies, and leadership are both informative and inspirational, reinforcing the idea that success can be measured not only by net worth but by influence and impact.

For those interested in luxury goods, Robb Report serves as the ultimate guide to high-end living. Known as "The Global Luxury Source," Robb Report covers everything from luxury watches and yachts to exclusive resorts and fine dining. An article on the latest Patek Philippe watch or a feature on a multimillion-dollar yacht is more than just a product review—it's an invitation to a lifestyle that most can only dream of. Robb Report doesn't just showcase luxury; it defines it, setting a standard for what it means to live a life of sophistication, exclusivity, and taste. For its readers, Robb Report is both a catalog of luxury and a source of inspiration, a reminder that wealth offers endless opportunities for indulgence and refinement.

Magazines like these play a pivotal role in shaping societal standards for wealth, creating a world where luxury is not only celebrated but idealized. By offering a curated view of high-end fashion, travel, and lifestyle, they influence readers' perceptions of what it means to be successful and stylish. For many, these magazines are not just publications—they're aspirational guides that reflect and reinforce the values of a society that equates wealth with worth.

Traditional media—through television, film, celebrity news, financial journalism, and print magazines—continues to play a powerful role in defining and celebrating wealth. These platforms don't just show the trappings of luxury; they explore the complexities of living with wealth, from the highs of power and influence to the lows of scrutiny and public critique. Through shows like Billions, news segments on Elon Musk's net worth, and Vogue covers featuring the rich and famous, traditional media constructs a narrative around wealth that is both aspirational and cautionary.

The portrayal of wealth in traditional media serves as a mirror to society's fascination with the elite, influencing how we view success, power, and lifestyle. In an age where social media has made wealth more accessible and visible than ever before, traditional media still holds sway, providing context, depth, and often a touch of glamour. These portrayals remind us that while wealth can open doors, it also brings challenges, responsibilities, and, sometimes, isolation.

As we continue to consume stories about the ultra-wealthy through traditional media, our understanding of wealth will keep evolving, shaped by narratives that make us question, aspire, and sometimes envy. In many ways, traditional media offers a timeless exploration of wealth and luxury—a reminder that, for better or worse, society will always be captivated by the power and allure of success.

# Chapter 4.6: Wealth and Social Media: A Double-Edged Sword

If there's one thing we know about social media, it's that it has the power to amplify anything it touches. From the latest sneaker drops to the most extravagant private islands, social media has a way of making everything feel larger-than-life and, at times, untouchable. For wealth, the impact is both fascinating and complex. Social media doesn't just showcase wealth—it redefines it, complicates it, and makes it available for everyone to see, critique, aspire to, and sometimes even envy. But with all that visibility comes an array of issues, especially for viewers who are just trying to understand what it means to be "successful."

## The Dark Side of Wealth Visibility: More Than Just Glossy Photos

Imagine scrolling through Instagram and seeing back-to-back posts of yachts, private jets, designer outfits, and fine dining experiences. Each photo is a carefully crafted image of a lifestyle many only dream about, and it's hard not to feel a pang of longing, or perhaps a touch of inadequacy, when every second post seems to scream, "Look at how well I'm doing!" These images, often tagged with hashtags like #blessed, #livingmybestlife, or #luxurylifestyle, project a sense of ease, freedom, and ultimate success.

But here's the twist: many of these posts show only a fraction of the full picture. Behind the designer bags, luxury getaways, and champagne-fueled sunsets are people dealing with a range of issues that rarely make it onto social feeds. Social media creates a highlight reel, not a documentary. This constant flow of high-gloss visuals can warp the perception of what wealth truly is, and how it's achieved. When viewers see endless luxury without the context of struggle, hard work, and even a touch of luck, they might begin to believe that wealth is easy to achieve—or worse, that they are somehow failing by not living a similar lifestyle.

## The Pressure of Perfection

Let's break down how this impacts viewers on a deeper level. Picture a young professional, scrolling through TikTok, Instagram, or YouTube. She sees influencers and celebrities casually sharing snippets of their lives that include penthouses, beach vacations, and the latest designer trends. There's an implication that this level of comfort and affluence is both expected and achievable. The problem? She's comparing her daily grind to their curated feeds. It's like looking at a flawless magazine cover and assuming you're not beautiful enough because you don't look exactly like the airbrushed model on the page. This is the dilemma of the digital age—except now, the "models" are people we believe to be "just like us" or at least people who achieved wealth seemingly overnight.

Now, add to that mix the influencers who make their money by promoting financial success as something anyone can achieve if they just "hustle" hard enough. Many of these "gurus" are selling courses, guides, or investments with promises of easy wealth. In reality, they're often making their money not through the methods they promote but by selling the idea of those methods to others. For many followers, this leads to a vicious cycle of pursuing financial "hacks" or shortcuts that rarely deliver on their promises. When these efforts inevitably fall short, followers might feel not just disappointed but also ashamed, wondering what's wrong with them for not seeing the same success.

## Mental Health Consequences: A Growing Concern

The impact of this unrealistic portrayal of wealth doesn't end at disappointment; it can have real mental health implications. Studies have shown that social media can contribute to feelings of anxiety, depression, and low self-esteem, especially when users are constantly exposed to the filtered lives of others. For many, the comparison game becomes impossible to escape, and when the target is a lifestyle rooted in extreme wealth, it's even harder to ignore.

There's an entire industry built around self-help, self-improvement, and financial growth, which can be incredibly positive—until it becomes toxic. Imagine someone who's constantly exposed to content that says, "If you're not rich, you're not working hard enough." This message, while not always overt, can be draining. It subtly suggests that wealth is the ultimate measure of personal worth, leading individuals to push themselves harder, sometimes beyond their limits, and to feel like failures if they don't reach that level of success. The danger here isn't just burnout; it's the possibility of losing sight of one's values, priorities, and sense of self-worth in the endless pursuit of an Instagram-worthy life.

## A Changing Definition of Wealth: Influence, Networks, and Lifestyle Choices

Wealth today isn't just about what's in your bank account; it's also about who you know, what you can influence, and how you live. This evolution is evident everywhere you look on social media. Nowadays, we don't just see billionaires as the only wealthy individuals—many people with influence, a large following, or a unique lifestyle are perceived as wealthy too. They might not have billions, but their influence over trends, brands, and consumer behavior gives them a cultural currency that's hard to quantify.

## The Rise of Social Capital: More Than Money

Consider a YouTube creator with millions of subscribers who reviews luxury cars, or a TikTok influencer who creates viral beauty tutorials. They might not be wealthy in the traditional sense, but they possess something valuable: social capital. Brands pay them to showcase their products, people look to them for opinions, and their followers emulate their lifestyle choices. This influence is its own form of wealth because it gives them a certain level of power, access, and respect within their niche.

Take for instance, lifestyle influencers who live in trendy, beautifully decorated apartments in popular cities. They may not have the funds to buy a mansion or take luxury vacations, but their aesthetic and lifestyle choices resonate with a large audience. People want to dress like them, eat where they eat, and buy what they recommend. This is a form of influence that doesn't require a massive bank account but instead relies on taste, presence, and the ability to connect with followers in a way that feels genuine. Brands have noticed this too, which is why influencer marketing has become a multi-billion dollar industry. In essence, these influencers hold wealth in their ability to direct attention, shape trends, and impact consumer behavior.

## Network as Wealth: Connections Count

We also see wealth today defined by one's network. The old saying, "It's not what you know, but who you know," has never been more accurate, especially in the world of social media. An entrepreneur with a modest income but with connections to other influential figures may have access to opportunities that others can only dream of. Social media has turned networking into a currency—followers, collaborators, and connections can open doors that money alone can't.

Think about platforms like LinkedIn, where professionals with large networks can share insights, launch products, and receive immediate feedback from thousands of other professionals. A single post from a well-connected individual can generate leads, attract job offers, or even inspire new business ideas. This type of wealth, grounded in relationships and reputation, is invaluable in the digital age. It means that someone's worth isn't solely based on their financial assets but also on the opportunities they can create or influence through their connections.

## Lifestyle as a Status Symbol: Not Just What You Own, But How You Live

Finally, wealth is being defined by lifestyle choices that communicate a sense of individuality and sophistication. In an era when experiences often hold more value than possessions, the way one lives has become a new marker of wealth. Social media allows people to share every detail of their lives—from the exotic places they travel to the unique hobbies they pursue and the art they collect. In this context, wealth is seen as living a life filled with unique, meaningful experiences, not just material items.

Consider the trend of "digital nomads" who live and work around the world. They may not have a single physical asset, but their lifestyle—moving from Bali to Tokyo to Lisbon, working remotely from coffee shops or beaches—embodies a type of freedom and flexibility that many equate with wealth. This is a kind of social media-driven rebranding of wealth, where it's not just about assets but about how those assets allow one to live. The luxury here is freedom—the freedom to work from anywhere, to design one's own schedule, to avoid the conventional nine-to-five. This ability to lead a life full of travel and independence has become a new aspirational symbol of wealth.

# Wealth, Society, and a New American Dream

For generations, the "American Dream" painted a familiar picture: a steady job, a modest home, and the promise of upward mobility. But in recent years, the idea of what it means to be successful, or even affluent, has started to shift. No longer confined to a select elite or the traditional paths of wealth—inheritance, corporate empires, or elite education—today's wealth creation is more diverse, more accessible, and often less predictable. We're in a moment where financial success has slipped out of the exclusive grip of the 1% and started to spread into new territories, reaching people from all walks of life, backgrounds, and skill sets.

This isn't to say the American Dream is gone; rather, it's evolving. Technology, social media, and personal branding have rewritten the rules of wealth creation, allowing people to take ownership of their financial futures in ways that would have been unimaginable a few decades ago. Imagine the influencers who turn their hobbies into six-figure incomes, the entrepreneurs who launch online businesses with nothing more than a laptop, or the young investors mastering stock portfolios through smartphone apps. Wealth is no longer strictly about what's handed down or locked behind closed doors. Instead, it's about tapping into opportunities that can be just as accessible to someone from a small town as they are to someone born into privilege.

Let's dive into this new landscape of wealth, where financial goals are as much a part of popular culture as they are a personal aspiration. We'll examine how pathways to affluence are expanding, empowering millions to chase their own version of financial freedom and redefining what it means to be "wealthy" in the process. Here, we're exploring a new era where wealth doesn't just belong to a select few; it's something people from all backgrounds can pursue and, in many cases, achieve.

## Chapter 5.1: The Digital Revolution: Unlocking New Pathways to Wealth

In the last decade, technology has cracked open doors to financial opportunities that were once locked tight for most people. Wealth-building used to require insider knowledge, considerable initial investment, and access to elite networks. Now, thanks to the digital revolution, nearly anyone with a smartphone and an internet connection can start investing, saving, and even lending money in ways that would have been unthinkable just a generation ago. From investing apps that put Wall Street in your pocket to cryptocurrencies that bypass traditional banks, we're witnessing an explosion of new ways to create wealth. And it's not just the ultra-wealthy getting in on the action; today's financial landscape is inviting everyone—from college students to retired grandparents—to join the journey.

### The Rise of Digital Finance: Wealth in the Palm of Your Hand

Imagine the world of investing 30 years ago. If you wanted to invest in stocks, bonds, or mutual funds, you'd likely need to go through a financial advisor, open an account with a brokerage firm, and pony up a significant amount of money just to get started. It was a world with high barriers—both in terms of knowledge and capital. Fast forward to today, and the rise of digital finance has transformed that world entirely. Now, with just a few taps on your phone, you can start building wealth, regardless of your income level or experience.

## Robinhood and the Power of Commission-Free Trading

Robinhood was one of the first platforms to bring commission-free trading to the masses, and it changed the game entirely. Commission fees, which could range from $5 to $10 per trade, used to be a major barrier for small-time investors. Let's say you had $100 to invest and paid a $10 fee—right away, you've lost 10% of your investment just for the privilege of getting in the game. But with Robinhood's zero-commission model, that $100 can be fully invested in stocks, ETFs, or even options, making it easier than ever to dip a toe into the stock market.

Picture a college student who's saved up $50 from her part-time job and wants to invest. A decade ago, that $50 would have hardly been enough to cover the minimum investment requirements, let alone fees. Today, she can use it to buy a fraction of a share in her favorite tech company, check her portfolio every day, and learn the ropes of investing as she goes along. This hands-on experience, made possible by platforms like Robinhood, empowers people to start building wealth early in life, even if they're only starting with pocket change.

## Acorns: Turning Spare Change into Wealth

Acorns takes a different approach to investing by turning spare change into an investment opportunity. This app rounds up purchases to the nearest dollar and invests the difference, so each time you buy a coffee for $4.50, Acorns automatically rounds it up to $5.00 and invests that 50 cents in a diversified portfolio. This "set it and forget it" model is ideal for people who might feel intimidated by investing or who think they don't have enough money to make a difference.

Imagine a young professional who's still paying off student loans and thinks there's no room in her budget for investing. Acorns allows her to get started with tiny amounts, so she can begin to grow her money with zero effort on her part. Over time, those small amounts add up, creating a snowball effect that can lead to substantial savings and investments down the road.

## Wealthfront: Robo-Advisors for Everyone

Wealthfront takes the concept of financial planning to a whole new level by offering automated investment management through robo-advisors. Traditionally, a personalized investment plan would require hiring a financial advisor—a luxury that many people simply couldn't afford. Wealthfront and similar platforms democratize this service by using algorithms to create and manage a diversified portfolio tailored to the user's risk tolerance and goals.

For instance, let's consider a recent college graduate who's starting his first full-time job. He knows he should be investing for the future but doesn't have the time or expertise to research stocks and build a portfolio. By signing up for Wealthfront, he gets an automated investment plan that adjusts over time based on his financial goals. The best part? The fees are minimal compared to a traditional financial advisor, allowing him to maximize his returns without breaking the bank.

Together, these platforms—Robinhood, Acorns, Wealthfront, and many others—have turned investing into something that anyone can access. For the first time, we're seeing a truly democratic approach to building wealth, where people at every income level can start growing their money and setting themselves up for financial success.

## Cryptocurrency and Blockchain: A Whole New Way to Build Wealth

While investing apps have opened up the stock market to the masses, perhaps the most groundbreaking development in recent years has been the rise of cryptocurrency. Bitcoin, Ethereum, Solana, and thousands of other digital currencies have created new avenues for wealth creation that operate outside the traditional financial system. But it's not just the currencies themselves that have shaken things up—it's the underlying blockchain technology, which allows for secure, transparent transactions without the need for banks or middlemen.

## Bitcoin and the Birth of Digital Gold

Bitcoin, the first cryptocurrency, was introduced in 2009 as a decentralized digital currency, and it quickly earned the nickname "digital gold." Why? Because, like gold, it's finite—only 21 million Bitcoins will ever be created, which gives it a scarcity that drives up its value over time. For early adopters, Bitcoin presented an unprecedented opportunity: with just an internet connection, anyone could buy into this new form of currency and potentially ride its waves of volatility to enormous returns.

Consider the story of a software engineer who, in 2011, used $100 to buy Bitcoin when it was priced around $1. Fast-forward to 2021, and each Bitcoin is worth tens of thousands of dollars, transforming that $100 into a life-changing sum. Stories like these have captivated the public and brought millions of people into the world of cryptocurrency, all driven by the potential for massive returns and the promise of a decentralized financial future.

## Ethereum and the Rise of Smart Contracts

Ethereum took blockchain technology a step further by introducing "smart contracts," which are self-executing contracts with the terms of the agreement directly written into code. This innovation opened the door to decentralized applications (dApps) that could operate independently of any central authority. Now, developers could create games, financial services, and marketplaces on the blockchain, all powered by Ethereum.

Imagine a young entrepreneur who wants to launch a new app but doesn't want to go through traditional funding channels. With Ethereum, she can create a dApp, raise funds through a decentralized model, and reach an audience directly. This kind of freedom and accessibility has made Ethereum a powerful tool for innovation and wealth creation, drawing in developers, investors, and users alike.

## The Role of Decentralized Finance (DeFi): A New Era of Banking

One of the most revolutionary offshoots of blockchain technology has been the rise of decentralized finance, or DeFi. Through DeFi platforms, people can access financial services like lending, borrowing, and earning interest without going through a bank or other intermediary. DeFi operates on blockchain networks, allowing users to manage their own assets, make direct transactions, and participate in a financial ecosystem without the fees and restrictions of traditional institutions.

Think about the experience of someone living in a country with limited access to banking. Through DeFi, they can lend or borrow cryptocurrency, earn interest, and even exchange assets—all without needing a bank account. For many people in developing regions, DeFi represents the first time they've had true control over their finances. And for younger generations in wealthier countries, DeFi is a compelling alternative to the traditional banking system, with its promises of high returns and low barriers to entry.

## Financial Education and Accessibility: Knowledge is Power

One of the most exciting aspects of the digital revolution in finance is the increased accessibility to financial knowledge. In the past, understanding concepts like investing, budgeting, or retirement planning often required a financial advisor, a college education, or hours spent reading thick, jargon-filled books. Now, all of that has changed. Thanks to YouTube, podcasts, TikTok, and other social media platforms, financial education is at everyone's fingertips.

## YouTube and Podcasts: Learning the Ropes

YouTube and podcasts have become gold mines for financial education. Creators including Graham Stephan, Andrei Jikh, and channels like The Financial Diet offer in-depth discussions on personal finance, investing, and even taxes, making complex financial topics accessible and engaging. These creators often share their own experiences, including mistakes they've made and lessons they've learned, making finance feel relatable instead of intimidating.

Imagine a recent college grad who wants to start saving for retirement but has no idea where to begin. Instead of meeting with an expensive advisor, she can watch YouTube videos that break down the basics of 401(k)s, Roth IRAs, and investing strategies. This access to knowledge, presented in an easy-to-understand format, empowers her to make informed decisions about her financial future without ever leaving her couch.

## TikTok and the Rise of "Finfluencers"

Then there's TikTok, where "finfluencers" share bite-sized financial tips in videos that are often just 60 seconds long. For younger audiences, TikTok's format is ideal: it's fast, to the point, and surprisingly informative. Influencers Humphrey Yang and Tori Dunlap have millions of followers who tune in to learn about everything from building credit to investing in stocks.

For a high school student who's curious about finance, TikTok is a perfect entry point. In just a few minutes a day, he can pick up tips on saving money, building credit, or budgeting, all while scrolling through his feed. This exposure to financial literacy from a young age plants seeds that can grow into strong financial habits later in life.

## Financial Education for All: The Democratizing Power of Knowledge

The democratization of financial knowledge has huge implications for wealth-building. When financial education is accessible to everyone, people are better equipped to make smart decisions, avoid scams, and take advantage of opportunities. For many, learning about finance through these platforms represents the first time they've felt confident in managing their money, investing, or planning for the future.

In today's world, knowledge truly is power. And with so much financial information readily available, millions of people are discovering that they, too, can participate in wealth-building, regardless of their background or income level.

## Conclusion: A New Era of Wealth-Building

The digital revolution has fundamentally transformed the landscape of wealth-building. Through user-friendly apps, decentralized currencies, and accessible financial education, people from all backgrounds now have pathways to financial success that were once unimaginable. Whether it's investing spare change through Acorns, trading cryptocurrency, or learning about money management on TikTok, the barriers to financial participation are falling fast.

This new era of wealth democratization has created a culture where financial ambition is no longer a privilege—it's an expectation. As we look to the future, it's clear that digital finance is not just a trend; it's a powerful force reshaping the world of wealth and opening doors for millions of people to redefine what financial success means to them. For the first time in history, the opportunity to build wealth is truly in the hands of the many, not the few. And that's a revolution worth paying attention to.

## Chapter 5.2: Social Media and the Cult of the Self-Made Millionaire

In the age of Instagram, YouTube, and TikTok, the idea of the "self-made millionaire" has taken on a whole new life. Gone are the days when building wealth required decades of hard work in traditional industries or navigating the corporate ladder. Today, anyone with a smartphone, a unique voice, and a bit of charisma can potentially build a fortune online. As we have discussed, social media has democratized access to wealth creation, giving millions of people the tools to cultivate personal brands, grow audiences, and monetize their skills or passions in ways that were unthinkable just a few years ago.

But this digital gold rush has also brought with it a unique culture around wealth—a cult of the self-made millionaire that blends the allure of financial independence with a relentless "hustle" mentality. Whether it's fitness influencers selling workout programs, tech entrepreneurs promoting startups, or lifestyle bloggers sharing their latest sponsorships, social media is brimming with the stories of people who have seemingly cracked the code to financial success. And in many ways, these stories have become blueprints for anyone hoping to achieve similar success. Let's dive into how social media has fueled the rise of this cult of self-made wealth and what it means for our collective views on affluence.

## The Rise of Social Media Millionaires: Wealth-Building in the Digital Age

The idea of becoming wealthy through social media might have sounded absurd a decade ago, but today, it's common to see people building fortunes entirely online. Instagram, YouTube, TikTok, and Twitch offer anyone a stage—and potentially, an income stream. By sharing their lives, talents, or knowledge, countless people have transformed their followings into thriving businesses.

## The Business of Influence: Monetizing Passion and Personality

One of the most fascinating aspects of social media wealth-building is how ordinary people can turn their personal lives into profitable brands. Take, for example, a fitness influencer who starts by sharing simple workout tips on Instagram. As her following grows, she begins to receive offers from brands to promote protein powders, workout gear, and supplements. From there, she might launch her own line of fitness apparel or online workout programs, parlaying her initial popularity into a full-fledged business.

Take Kayla Itsines, an Australian fitness trainer who started by posting workout videos on Instagram. Her "Sweat" app, which offers workout plans and nutrition guides, has become a multi-million dollar empire. It's a remarkable example of how social media has enabled people not just to reach global audiences, but to monetize their influence directly. Whether it's through ads, product lines, or premium content, these influencers are proof that anyone with expertise, personality, or a unique voice can turn their passion into a lucrative business.

## YouTube and the Power of Niche Communities

YouTube has been a game-changer for aspiring entrepreneurs. Unlike traditional media, where screen time and roles are often limited to a select few, YouTube allows anyone to upload videos and build an audience. Marques Brownlee (MKBHD), who reviews tech gadgets, or Emma Chamberlain, who vlogs her daily life, have turned their channels into major brands. They reach millions, make substantial ad revenue, land sponsorships, and build loyal fan bases—all without ever having to go through traditional media gatekeepers.

Consider the example of Graham Stephan, a former real estate agent who started a YouTube channel to share his experiences and financial advice. By consistently posting videos investing, saving, and real estate, he grew his audience into the millions and now earns a significant income through ad revenue, sponsorships, and other business ventures. For his followers, Graham represents the ideal of the self-made millionaire—someone who didn't start with massive wealth but built it through a combination of smarts, consistency, and online reach.

## TikTok and the Rapid Rise of Influencers

TikTok has brought a fresh wave of influencers into the spotlight, many of whom have reached stardom seemingly overnight. Charli D'Amelio, started by posting dance videos, and within months, she became one of the platform's most-followed creators, leading to sponsorship deals, brand collaborations, and even a Dunkin' Donuts drink named after her. TikTok's short-form video format makes it easy for users to get discovered, and for those with an engaging presence, this discovery can translate quickly into fame—and wealth.

But it's not just the mega-famous who are profiting. Smaller creators can also monetize through brand partnerships, affiliate marketing, and even virtual "gifts" from followers. This model allows creators of all sizes to earn, even if they don't have millions of followers. For instance, a beauty enthusiast with a modest following might receive sponsorship offers from skincare brands or free products to review. The ability to monetize a niche audience is one of the defining features of today's social media landscape, and it's part of what makes wealth-building on these platforms so accessible.

## Aspirational Wealth and the "Hustle Culture": The Rise of Self-Made Role Models

One of the dominant messages circulating on social media is that anyone can achieve financial success if they're willing to work hard enough. This concept, often referred to as "hustle culture," has been popularized by high-profile figures such as Gary Vaynerchuk, Grant Cardone, and Rachelle Robinson. These influencers and entrepreneurs promote the idea that wealth is within reach of anyone willing to hustle, innovate, and take risks. They share not just business strategies, but also motivational content encouraging followers to work longer, network harder, and think bigger.

## Gary Vaynerchuk: The King of the Hustle Mindset

Gary Vaynerchuk, or "Gary Vee," as he's known to his fans, is a prime example of the hustle culture mentality. A serial entrepreneur and CEO of VaynerMedia, he gained popularity through YouTube videos and social media posts where he shares blunt, no-nonsense advice on business and life. His mantra? Work harder than everyone else, leverage social media, and don't make excuses.

Gary's story is compelling because he didn't come from wealth. He built his brand by transforming his family's wine business and then moving into digital marketing, amassing a fortune along the way. His appeal lies in his relatability—he's upfront about his struggles and doesn't sugarcoat the work involved in building a business. For his followers, Gary Vee represents the ultimate self-made success story, one that seems attainable as long as you're willing to grind.

## The Allure of the Side Hustle

In addition to promoting relentless work ethics, hustle culture has also popularized the concept of the "side hustle." Social media is filled with stories of people who start small businesses, take on freelance work, or build online stores while still working a 9-to-5 job. From Etsy shops to drop shipping stores, these side hustles are often portrayed as stepping stones to financial freedom.

Take, for example, Rachelle Robinson, a social media influencer who turned her passion for personal development into a business. She started by sharing tips on time management and productivity, and eventually launched a series of online courses and coaching programs. Through her story, Rachelle inspires followers to take their interests seriously and pursue side projects that might one day replace their day jobs. For many people, the side hustle is more than just extra income—it's a chance to build something of their own and move closer to the dream of financial independence.

## Influencers as Modern Wealth Icons: Redefining the American Dream

Social media influencers have become symbols of affluence in their own right, and their success stories challenge traditional notions of wealth. Unlike the old model, where wealth was primarily tied to family inheritance, elite education, or corporate power, influencers build wealth by leveraging their personalities, lifestyles, and online followings. Figures like Kylie Jenner and Kim Kardashian have shown that digital space can serve as a springboard to immense wealth, blurring the line between celebrity and entrepreneurship.

## Kylie Jenner: From Social Media to Billionaire Status

Kylie Jenner's rise to billionaire status through her beauty brand, Kylie Cosmetics, is one of the most striking examples of wealth-building through social media. Jenner leveraged her massive Instagram following to launch and promote her beauty products, bypassing traditional advertising channels and reaching consumers directly. Her success showed that personal branding and social media influence could build a billion-dollar business—a revelation that inspired countless others to follow a similar path.

For her followers, Kylie's success is both aspirational and tangible. She represents a new kind of wealth, one that's tied not to a corporate legacy or inherited fortune, but to the ability to connect with an audience and sell directly to them. Kylie's journey has redefined what it means to be a "self-made" billionaire, challenging traditional notions of affluence and inspiring a generation to see social media as a potential pathway to wealth.

## Kim Kardashian: Blending Celebrity with Entrepreneurship

Kim Kardashian has also redefined wealth in the digital age, turning her social media presence into a multi-million dollar empire. With KKW Beauty, Skims, and her various endorsement deals, Kim has monetized her personal brand in ways that are unprecedented. She uses social media not just to connect with fans, but to promote her businesses, engage with her audience, and solidify her position as a modern wealth icon.

For many of her followers, Kim represents a new form of financial independence—one that doesn't require a corporate job or even a traditional business background. She's proof that, in today's world, wealth can be built on the strength of one's brand and connection to an audience. Kim's success has paved the way for countless influencers and creators who see her as proof that they, too, can build wealth by cultivating their own unique identities online.

## Crowdfunding and Crowdsourced Wealth: The Power of Collective Support

Another critical way social media has democratized wealth is through crowdfunding platforms Kickstarter, GoFundMe, and Patreon. These platforms allow individuals to raise money for creative projects, business ideas, and even personal causes, tapping into the collective power of their audience to bring ideas to life.

## Kickstarter and the Growth of Niche Markets

Kickstarter, one of the earliest and most popular crowdfunding platforms, allows creators to pitch their projects to the public and receive funding from backers. This model has enabled countless entrepreneurs to launch businesses, products, and creative projects without relying on traditional investors or banks. For example, the creators of the popular card game "Exploding Kittens" raised over $8 million on Kickstarter, turning their idea into a successful business without any outside investors.

This type of funding allows creators to take risks and pursue niche markets that might not have been viable in a traditional investment environment. For the backers, crowdfunding offers a unique opportunity to support projects they're passionate about, becoming part of the journey rather than just being consumers. Crowdfunding has made it possible for anyone with a great idea and an engaged audience to build wealth from scratch.

## Patreon and the Rise of the Creator Economy

Patreon takes a different approach to crowdfunding by allowing creators to earn recurring revenue from their supporters, known as patrons.

Artists, writers, podcasters, and other creators can offer exclusive content to patrons in exchange for monthly support, creating a stable income stream that allows them to pursue their work full-time.

Consider an independent musician who uses Patreon to fund her music production. Without a record label, she might struggle to cover the costs of recording and promotion, but with Patreon, her fans can contribute directly, giving her the resources to continue creating. For patrons, this direct relationship with creators is deeply satisfying, as they're supporting the art and content they love. Patreon's model has empowered thousands of creators to make a living from their passions, proving that wealth can be built on creativity and community support.

## Conclusion: The Changing Face of the Self-Made Millionaire

The cult of the self-made millionaire has become a defining feature of social media culture, reshaping the American Dream for a new generation. Instagram, YouTube, and Patreon have turned wealth-building into a possibility for millions of people, making it more accessible than ever before. From influencers who monetize their personal brands to creators who crowdfund their projects, social media has opened up pathways to wealth that were once unimaginable.

In this new landscape, wealth is no longer just about bank accounts and assets—it's about influence, connection, and the ability to create value in real-time. This shift has empowered a generation to take control of their financial futures, challenging traditional ideas about who can become affluent and how. And while the journey of the self-made millionaire may be more accessible, it also reflects a broader change in how we define success, creativity, and ambition in the digital age.

# Chapter 5.3: Personal Branding: Building Wealth from Identity

When we think about wealth-building, we often imagine traditional routes: climbing the corporate ladder, starting a business, or investing in stocks. But in today's digital world, there's a new path to financial success that's not built on a résumé or a fancy degree. Instead, it's built on you—your story, your interests, and your unique voice. Personal branding has become a powerful way to create influence, foster connections, and generate income by simply sharing who you are. By cultivating a distinct identity that resonates with an audience, people are transforming their personalities, interests, and passions into thriving businesses.

## The Power of the Personal Brand: Turning Identity into Influence and Income

A personal brand is like a fingerprint; it's entirely unique to you. It's the story you tell about yourself and how you choose to share that story with the world. People follow influencers, read blogs, or watch YouTube channels not just for the content, but because they connect with the person behind it. A strong personal brand allows you to monetize that connection by attracting audiences, creating partnerships, and even launching products.

## Case Study: The Rise of Influencers with Daniel Wellington

One of the best-known examples of a brand that understood the power of personal branding is Daniel Wellington, a Swedish watch company. When they first entered the market, they didn't go the traditional route of running expensive ads or working with big celebrity endorsements. Instead, they partnered with social media influencers—people who had built strong personal brands around their lifestyles, aesthetics, and daily lives.

Imagine an influencer who posts daily about fashion and style. She has an Instagram feed that's beautifully curated, filled with her daily outfits, favorite accessories, and glimpses into her life. Her followers don't just care about her clothes; they care about her recommendations because she feels like a friend. When she posts a picture wearing a Daniel Wellington watch and shares a discount code, her followers trust her enough to make a purchase. By aligning with these influencers' personal brands, Daniel Wellington built a reputation that felt authentic and accessible, ultimately creating a global brand without ever using traditional advertising.

This strategy not only skyrocketed Daniel Wellington's growth, but it also allowed influencers to monetize their personal brands by earning commissions, increasing their visibility, and securing partnerships with other companies. It's a win-win that shows just how powerful personal branding can be as a wealth-building strategy for both individuals and companies.

## Case Study: Rachel Hollis and the Business of Authenticity

Rachel Hollis is another example of someone who leveraged personal branding to create significant wealth. Rachel started her career as an event planner and blogger, but she became widely known after sharing her personal stories of struggle and success on social media. With her approachable, down-to-earth style, she resonated with thousands of followers, especially women, who found her honesty refreshing. She didn't shy away from talking about her challenges as a working mom, her insecurities, and her path to self-confidence—all things that made her relatable.

Her personal brand took off after she published her book, Girl, Wash Your Face, which encouraged readers to embrace authenticity, ambition, and self-acceptance. Her success wasn't just about writing a book; it was about building a personal brand that inspired people. She used her platform to launch courses, host live events, and build a business empire that includes coaching and motivational speaking. Rachel Hollis showed that by embracing who you are and sharing your story, you can build not just a following, but a lucrative business based entirely on personal branding.

## The Global Reach of Personal Branding: From Local to International Audiences

One of the most amazing things about personal branding in the digital age is its global reach. Unlike traditional businesses, which often rely on local markets, personal branding allows you to connect with people from all over the world. Instagram, YouTube, and LinkedIn offer a global stage for anyone who's willing to put themselves out there. This means that even if you're starting from a modest background, you can still reach a massive audience.

Take, for example, Huda Kattan, a beauty influencer and founder of Huda Beauty. Huda began by posting makeup tutorials on YouTube, sharing her tips and techniques for achieving flawless looks. She was based in Dubai, but her personal brand quickly reached audiences far beyond the Middle East. Her unique approach and relatable personality attracted millions of followers, and eventually, she launched her own line of beauty products, which became an international sensation. Today, Huda Beauty is a multi-million dollar brand, and Huda Kattan is one of the most influential voices in the beauty industry—all because she used her personal brand to build a connection with a global audience.

## How Personal Branding Allows You to Create Multiple Streams of Income

One of the best parts about personal branding is that it doesn't just open up one door—it opens up several. Once you've built a following, you have a range of options for monetizing your influence. Some popular ways to turn a personal brand into income include:

**Brand Partnerships**: Many influencers partner with brands for sponsored posts, earning money by promoting products that align with their brand.

**Product Sales:** Once you have an audience, you can create your own products—anything from physical items, like skincare or apparel, to digital products, including e-books or online courses.

**Subscription-Based Content**: Platforms like Patreon allow creators to offer exclusive content to their most loyal followers for a monthly fee.

**Affiliate Marketing:** With affiliate marketing, you earn a commission by promoting products from other companies. If your followers purchase through your referral links, you earn a percentage of the sales.

**Ad Revenue:** YouTube and blogs with high traffic can generate significant income through ad revenue.

By diversifying their income streams, people with strong personal brands create more financial security and independence, turning their online personas into full-fledged businesses.

## Building Your Personal Brand: Finding Your Niche and Voice

Building a personal brand isn't about trying to appeal to everyone; it's about finding a niche and speaking directly to a specific audience. The most successful personal brands are authentic and consistent. Let's take a look at some steps that can help you develop your personal brand.

### Step 1: Identify Your Niche and Passion

The first step to building a personal brand is figuring out what makes you unique. What are you passionate about? What do you have expertise in? Your niche could be anything from fitness to finance, cooking to coding. The key is to find a topic you love enough to talk about consistently.

Consider someone like Marie Kondo, who built her brand around the idea of "sparking joy" through organization. She took a very specific niche—decluttering—and made it the foundation of her personal brand. Through her books, Netflix series, and social media, she's created a following of people who want to learn how to organize their lives in a way that brings happiness. By focusing on a specific topic and staying true to her philosophy, Marie has turned a niche into a global movement.

## Step 2: Develop a Unique Voice and Visual Identity

In personal branding, how you present yourself matters. This includes everything from the tone of your content to the colors and visuals you use. Think about the influencers and personalities you follow—chances are, they have a consistent style that makes them instantly recognizable.

Take Casey Neistat, for instance. The filmmaker and YouTuber is known for his unique storytelling style, gritty aesthetic, and high-energy videos. He's built a personal brand that's instantly recognizable, and his unique voice has attracted millions of followers. By developing a unique style, you make it easy for people to identify with your brand and feel connected to you.

## Step 3: Engage with Your Audience

Personal branding isn't just about talking to your followers; it's about talking with them. Engaging with your audience is one of the best ways to build a loyal community. Responding to comments, hosting Q&A sessions, or even just liking followers' posts can make people feel valued and connected to you.

Gary Vaynerchuk is known for responding to his followers on social media, whether it's a direct message, a comment, or a tweet. Gary takes the time to engage with his audience personally, which has helped him build a community of loyal followers who feel like they know him. This level of engagement can make a huge difference when building a personal brand; it shows people that you care about them and value their support.

## Step 4: Be Consistent and Authentic

Consistency is crucial in personal branding. If you start posting workout videos, your audience will expect fitness content. If you switch to talking about cooking the next day, you might confuse or lose your followers. Successful personal brands stay true to their core topics and values, allowing them to build a reliable and trustworthy presence online.

Authenticity is just as important. Followers can sense when someone is faking it, and they're less likely to trust a brand that feels inauthentic. Lifestyle influencer Jenna Kutcher is known for being open about her personal life, struggles, and successes. Her authenticity has made her relatable, and her followers feel like they're following a real person, not a curated persona. This level of honesty has made her brand not only successful but also impactful.

## Personal Branding as a Tool for Career Growth and Entrepreneurship

A strong personal brand isn't just valuable for influencers; it's also a powerful tool for anyone looking to advance in their career or start their own business. In the age of social media, a personal brand can make you stand out in a crowded job market or help you attract clients to your business.

## LinkedIn: Personal Branding for Professionals

LinkedIn is an excellent platform for building a professional personal brand. By sharing insights, engaging in conversations, and showcasing your expertise, you can position yourself as a thought leader in your industry. For instance, imagine a marketing professional who consistently shares tips on social media strategy and personal branding on LinkedIn. Over time, they build a following, get noticed by industry leaders, and attract job offers and consulting opportunities.

## Freelancers and Entrepreneurs: Building Trust Through Personal Branding

For freelancers and entrepreneurs, a personal brand can be a game-changer. When clients are choosing between different providers, a strong personal brand can be the deciding factor. A freelancer who consistently posts about their work, shares testimonials from clients, and offers insights into their creative process is likely to attract more business than one who doesn't.

Personal branding can also help small business owners stand out in their field. Imagine a graphic designer who regularly shares design tips and behind-the-scenes looks at her creative process on Instagram. By building a brand around her personality and work, she becomes more than just another designer—she becomes the go-to expert for clients who connect with her style and personality.

## Conclusion: Building Wealth by Being Yourself

Personal branding is a powerful tool that allows anyone, regardless of background, to turn their identity into influence and income. By finding a niche, developing a unique voice, and building authentic connections with an audience, people from all walks of life are transforming their personal brands into wealth-building machines.

In today's world, building wealth doesn't necessarily mean fitting into a traditional mold; it's about embracing who you are and sharing your journey with others. Whether you're an entrepreneur, an artist, or a professional, personal branding offers a unique opportunity to create financial success by simply being yourself. The digital age has shown us that wealth can come not just from what we do, but from who we are. And for many, that's an exciting, empowering way to redefine what it means to be successful.

## Chapter 5.4: Wealth Creation Beyond Traditional Professions

For much of history, the paths to wealth were relatively narrow and well-trodden. But times have changed, and so have the ways we can build financial security and prosperity. Thanks to technology and the internet, new doors have opened, allowing people to earn money outside the limits of traditional jobs or careers. Today, individuals are creating wealth through gig work, passive income, digital assets, and platforms that allow them to leverage their unique skills, assets, and time. Let's take a closer look at these modern wealth-building avenues that are empowering people around the globe to take financial control in ways that were once unimaginable.

### The Gig Economy and Wealth Expansion: A New Era of Small Business Owners

When most of us hear "gig economy," we might think of Uber drivers or freelance graphic designers. But the gig economy has come to encompass much more than just side gigs; it's become a legitimate pathway to financial freedom for many. Uber, Airbnb, Etsy, and Upwork have empowered people to turn their talents, assets, and time into money-making ventures. Essentially, these platforms allow almost anyone to become a small business owner without needing a physical storefront, a massive budget, or a big investor.

## Uber and Lyft: Driving Income on Your Own Terms

Imagine a teacher who wants to make some extra money over the summer. She's not interested in a second job with strict hours, but she could use a bit of supplemental income to cover some bills or take a well-deserved vacation. With Uber or Lyft, she can drive during her free time, setting her own schedule and picking up extra income on her terms. Over a few weeks, she earns enough to meet her financial goal, all without committing to a fixed part-time job.

The flexibility of the gig economy allows people to generate wealth on their own terms. Some drivers even work full-time with ride-sharing, transforming it into a primary income stream. In cities with high demand, experienced drivers who know the best times and places to work can earn impressive income. For many, this gig is about more than just money—it's about flexibility and control, things that traditional jobs often don't offer.

## Airbnb: Turning Homes into Income-Generating Assets

Another pillar of the gig economy is Airbnb, which has allowed homeowners and renters to earn money by renting out extra rooms or properties. Imagine a young couple who recently bought a house in a bustling city. They have an extra guest room that sits empty most of the time, so they decide to list it on Airbnb. Over time, the extra income from renting out the room on weekends helps them pay down their mortgage faster, providing a way to build equity and financial security.

For some, Airbnb becomes a primary income stream. People who own multiple properties often manage them exclusively as short-term rentals, earning substantial monthly income. Airbnb hosts, especially those in high-demand areas, are essentially running small hospitality businesses, and some even scale up by purchasing or managing additional properties to grow their earnings. The platform has turned real estate into a viable income source, even for those who may not have initially seen themselves as landlords.

## Etsy and Upwork: Creative and Professional Freedom

Etsy and Upwork are perfect examples of platforms that allow people to leverage unique skills to generate wealth. On Etsy, artists, jewelry makers, and crafters can sell handmade goods directly to consumers, bypassing the need for retail partnerships or brick-and-mortar stores. For example, a stay-at-home parent with a passion for crafting might start by selling handmade candles or custom jewelry on Etsy. As sales grow, what began as a small hobby can turn into a full-fledged business, with loyal customers and a steady income.

Similarly, Upwork has transformed freelance work by providing a platform where professionals in fields like writing, design, programming, and marketing can connect with clients globally. A talented graphic designer who prefers to work remotely can find steady projects through Upwork, earning income without the need for a traditional employer. These platforms offer users the freedom to set their own rates, choose their clients, and build reputations as independent contractors. For some freelancers, gig work is more than just a side hustle—it's a viable and often lucrative career path.

Together, these platforms have democratized access to wealth-building opportunities, making it possible for anyone with marketable skills or assets to become a small business owner. Unlike traditional paths, where wealth creation often depended on capital or connections, the gig economy has made financial independence accessible to a much broader audience.

## The Role of Passive Income and Digital Assets: Building Wealth in Your Sleep

The idea of earning money while you sleep sounds too good to be true, but for many people today, it's a reality. Passive income refers to money earned with minimal active involvement, and it has become one of the most attractive wealth-building strategies in the modern era. Whether through digital assets, investments, or automated businesses, people are increasingly finding ways to generate income streams that don't require a traditional job.

## Real Estate: A Classic Source of Passive Income

One of the most popular forms of passive income has always been real estate. For many, buying a property and renting it out is an effective way to generate monthly income without needing to work a nine-to-five job. A young professional might purchase a small condo as an investment, renting it out and using the rental income to cover the mortgage payments. Over time, as the property appreciates in value and the mortgage balance decreases, the condo becomes a valuable asset, providing both equity and a source of income.

Real estate investment trusts (REITs) offer another way to earn passive income from real estate without having to buy physical property. A REIT is essentially a company that owns, operates, or finances real estate, and by investing in it, individuals can earn dividends from real estate profits without the hassle of being a landlord. This allows people who may not have the capital to buy a property to still benefit from the real estate market.

## Digital Products: Earning from E-Books, Courses, and Content

Digital products have become an incredibly popular source of passive income, especially for entrepreneurs, creators, and influencers. Unlike physical products, which require inventory, shipping, and production costs, digital products can be created once and sold repeatedly. A blogger, for instance, might write an e-book on effective blogging strategies and sell it on their website. Each sale generates revenue without any additional work required, aside from occasional updates to keep the information current.

Online courses are another powerful digital asset. Take someone with expertise in photography who creates an online course on the basics of digital photography. By recording videos and creating course materials once, they can sell access to the course for years, generating income long after the initial work is complete. Udemy, Skillshare, and Teachable make it easy for anyone with knowledge to share to reach a global audience.

Passive income from digital products allows people to monetize their knowledge, skills, and passions in a way that scales effortlessly. It's an ideal option for those who want to create wealth outside of traditional jobs because it doesn't require constant effort to generate income once the product is live.

## Affiliate Marketing: Getting Paid for Promoting Products

Affiliate marketing is another popular source of passive income that has grown in the digital age. It involves promoting products from other companies and earning a commission on any sales generated through your referral links. Bloggers, YouTubers, and influencers often use affiliate links to recommend products they genuinely love, earning money each time a follower makes a purchase through their link.

For example, a travel blogger might join an affiliate program for a luggage brand, including links in their blog posts about travel essentials. If readers click on those links and buy the recommended luggage, the blogger earns a commission. Affiliate marketing works particularly well for those who have established trust with an audience, as people are more likely to purchase products recommended by someone they follow and admire.

Amazon Associates, ShareASale, and Impact make it easy for individuals to start earning through affiliate marketing, even without a massive following. With time and consistency, affiliate marketing can generate a steady stream of income, allowing people to benefit from product sales without the need for physical inventory or customer service.

## Digital Assets and Cryptocurrencies: Building Wealth Through Innovation

In addition to traditional investments, the rise of digital assets and cryptocurrencies has created new ways for people to build wealth. Unlike stocks or real estate, digital assets operate within the online world, offering unique opportunities and risks for those looking to expand their wealth.

## Cryptocurrencies: Bitcoin, Ethereum, and Beyond

Bitcoin and Ethereum have become popular investment options due to their potential for high returns. Unlike traditional currencies, which are managed by governments and banks, cryptocurrencies operate on decentralized blockchain technology, making them immune to traditional financial controls. This has attracted millions of people who view crypto as a way to build wealth outside the traditional banking system.

Consider a software engineer who invested a small amount in Bitcoin back in 2011 when it was worth only a few dollars. Fast forward a decade, and that small investment could now be worth a substantial amount, showcasing the potential for life-changing wealth. However, cryptocurrencies are notoriously volatile, and their value can swing wildly, making them a high-risk, high-reward investment.

For many, cryptocurrency represents an exciting opportunity to build wealth without the restrictions of traditional finance. While some people trade crypto actively, others choose to buy and hold, believing in the long-term value of blockchain technology. Regardless of the strategy, cryptocurrencies have introduced a new form of wealth-building that's unlike anything the financial world has seen before.

## NFTs and Digital Art: The New Frontier of Digital Assets

Another digital asset making waves is the non-fungible token, or NFT. NFTs are unique digital items—often artwork or collectibles—that are bought, sold, and traded on blockchain platforms. Unlike cryptocurrencies, NFTs are one-of-a-kind, meaning no two NFTs are the same.

Digital artist Beeple made headlines in 2021 when he sold an NFT of his artwork for over $69 million at a Christie's auction. This sale put NFTs on the map as a potentially lucrative asset class, and since then, countless artists, musicians, and creators have started producing NFTs as a way to sell their work directly to collectors. Imagine a musician who creates an exclusive album and releases it as an NFT, allowing a limited number of fans to own a piece of music history.

NFTs have given rise to a new kind of wealth-building, allowing artists to monetize their work in ways that were never possible before. And for collectors, NFTs represent a form of digital ownership that has the potential for long-term value appreciation.

## Redefining Wealth Creation: Moving Beyond Traditional Professions

What all these new avenues for wealth creation have in common is that they break the mold of traditional professions. In the past, wealth was typically concentrated among those with established careers or business ventures, but today, nearly anyone with an internet connection, a smartphone, and some creativity can start building wealth. This democratization of wealth creation has empowered millions of people to pursue financial independence on their own terms, without relying on traditional jobs.

The ability to generate income through gig work, passive investments, and digital assets has opened up a world of opportunities for people who want to chart their own path. For those who may not fit into traditional career roles or who crave the flexibility to work on their own terms, these new forms of wealth creation offer an exciting alternative.

## Embracing a New Era of Financial Freedom

The digital age has ushered in a new era of wealth creation, one where opportunities are no longer limited to a select few. Through gig work, passive income streams, and digital assets, millions of people have found ways to build wealth beyond the constraints of traditional professions. This shift has democratized access to financial success, allowing individuals from all backgrounds to leverage their skills, creativity, and resources to create financial independence.

As we move forward, the traditional paths to wealth may continue to evolve, but one thing is clear: wealth creation is no longer confined to boardrooms and corporate ladders. It's happening on the streets, online, and in homes around the world. The future of wealth is about flexibility, innovation, and empowerment. And for those willing to embrace this new landscape, financial freedom is more accessible than ever before.

## Conclusion: Embracing the Potential and Addressing the Challenges

The democratization of wealth has opened exciting new doors, expanding the ways people can pursue financial success beyond the traditional career path. But along with these opportunities come challenges, from the unrealistic promises of instant riches to the persistent inequalities of the digital divide. As we continue to explore and refine this new era of wealth creation, it's vital to stay aware of both the possibilities and the limitations.

For many, the allure of digital finance, social media, and personal branding is the dream of financial freedom on one's own terms. But achieving that dream takes more than just ambition—it takes knowledge, resilience, and a balanced perspective. By acknowledging the challenges of wealth democratization and working to overcome them, we can help ensure that the new economy serves as a genuine path to prosperity for all, not just a privileged few.

# Celebrity Wealth and the Role of Influence in the New Era

Once upon a time, wealth felt like a distant dream for most people—a world removed, inhabited by families with dynastic fortunes, high-powered business tycoons, and political elites. The average person might have glimpsed a lavish lifestyle on TV or in the pages of glossy magazines, but it was understood as something rare, out of reach, and reserved for an elite few. Wealth was a privilege, often passed down through generations or earned through traditional industries like finance, real estate, or high-stakes corporate roles. The idea of becoming wealthy, especially for those outside of established circles, felt abstract, like something that happened in another reality.

But fast forward to today, and that divide isn't so stark anymore. In the age of social media, wealth is now everywhere we look, from our Instagram feeds to YouTube channels, Twitter, and TikTok. A major shift has occurred: celebrity culture has moved from exclusive red carpets and secretive private estates to our screens, where celebrities, influencers, and social media personalities showcase their lives with remarkable accessibility. Celebrities aren't just seen in movies, music videos, or carefully curated photoshoots—they're part of our daily scroll, giving us seemingly unscripted glimpses into their lives, wealth, and success. Through this constant stream of content, the wealthy lifestyle has started to feel closer, more attainable, and perhaps even achievable.

In this chapter, we'll explore how celebrities shape our perceptions of wealth, influence our financial goals, and create a new kind of aspiration for affluence that feels both visible and accessible. From A-list actors and Grammy-winning musicians to YouTubers, TikTok stars, and Instagram influencers, the definition of "celebrity" has broadened dramatically. And with it, our ideas about what it means to be rich have shifted too. We're no longer just watching the rich live their lives from afar; we're seeing the lavish vacations, designer wardrobes, million-dollar mansions, and luxury cars in real-time—and with captions that tell us exactly where to buy, how to recreate, and, ultimately, how to aspire to that same lifestyle.

## The Rise of Celebrity Influence: Making Wealth Visible

In many ways, social media has redefined the very concept of celebrity. In the past, becoming famous required access to a small number of powerful industries: film, television, sports, or maybe music. Today, anyone with a smartphone and a unique voice can build an audience, become an influencer, and enter the world of fame and affluence.

Influencers have done more than just build their own wealth—they've changed how we think about wealth itself. When we watch Kylie Jenner on Instagram or Emma Chamberlain on YouTube, it feels personal, like we're seeing into their lives in a way that we never could with the old Hollywood stars. They give us behind-the-scenes glimpses, from their morning skincare routines to their home tours, showcasing luxury items as part of their everyday. By doing so, they've made wealth more visible and relatable, creating a sense of intimacy that fosters connection—and, for many followers, aspiration.

## The New Aspiration: Lifestyle of the Rich and "Relatable"

This accessibility of wealth has reshaped the classic "rags to riches" dream into something more immediate and personal. The influence of celebrity wealth isn't just about flaunting expensive things; it's about making those things feel achievable. When influencers share how they reached success or post about their business ventures, it gives followers the impression that they, too, can achieve that level of financial freedom. Celebrities and influencers alike often share "before and after" stories, narrating their rise from humble beginnings or past struggles, which makes the lifestyle they're now living feel like a potential path rather than an unattainable fantasy.

This relatability is even more pronounced with influencers who were once regular social media users just like their followers. The rise of TikTok stars Charli D'Amelio and Addison Rae, who amassed fame and wealth through their relatable personalities and viral dance videos, serves as proof that ordinary people can become rich and famous almost overnight. For young audiences, watching someone their age go from a high school student to a millionaire through TikTok videos feels attainable—if not immediate, then at least possible.

## The Influence of Celebrity Wealth on Financial Aspirations

The influence of celebrities on public financial aspirations is far-reaching. As they showcase their designer clothes, exotic vacations, and luxury homes, celebrities also create a roadmap of what success looks like, subtly shifting our perception of what it means to "make it." This visibility has inspired new generations to aspire not just for steady jobs and financial stability, but for the potential of millionaire lifestyles and passive income streams. Today's young adults and teens are growing up seeing influencers their age who have made fortunes, which affects how they think about wealth and career paths. The allure of entrepreneurship, influencer marketing, and self-made wealth is more appealing than ever.

Take the example of luxury beauty lines launched by celebrities like Rihanna with Fenty Beauty or Kim Kardashian with KKW Beauty. These brands have shown followers that they can parlay their passions into profitable businesses, blurring the lines between personal branding and entrepreneurship. The message? Wealth isn't limited to climbing the corporate ladder or securing a traditional job; it can come from building a brand based on who you are and what you love.

## Blurring the Lines Between the Wealthy and the Everyday Consumer

As celebrities make their wealth visible and seemingly attainable, they also change how the general public engages with luxury. Thanks to social media, luxury items aren't exclusively for the ultra-rich. With "dupes" or lookalikes, followers can feel like they're participating in the same lifestyle at a fraction of the cost. When influencers post about their skincare routines using expensive products, followers can often find similar options that feel more accessible. Even high-end brands have taken note, creating "entry-level" products that offer a taste of luxury without the hefty price tag.

The concept of "affordable luxury" has reshaped how people view wealth and spending. Followers might not be able to afford a celebrity's mansion, but they can buy the celebrity-endorsed face mask, gym outfit, or drink at Starbucks. This approach has given rise to a consumer culture where aspiring to wealth is less about the total amount in one's bank account and more about adopting certain pieces of the lifestyle.

## Setting the Stage for Celebrity Wealth and Influence

As we move forward, we'll explore how celebrities have not only redefined wealth but have also become role models for financial ambition, self-branding, and the pursuit of influence. Their visibility has made wealth seem closer, sparking both aspiration and questions about what it truly means to be successful in today's world. Celebrities have created an intersection between aspiration and accessibility, offering followers a window into a world that used to feel locked behind velvet ropes. This chapter dives deeper into the impact of celebrity wealth, examining how these influential figures shape our goals, values, and perceptions of what it means to be wealthy in the modern age.

## Chapter 6.1: The New Era of Celebrity Wealth

When we think about wealth and fame, images of old Hollywood stars, professional athletes, and renowned musicians often come to mind—people who seemed larger than life and were largely inaccessible to the general public. Figures like Elizabeth Taylor, Michael Jackson, and Jacqueline Kennedy Onassis defined what it meant to be rich and famous. Their lives were glamorous, and their wealth was a distant dream for most of us, visible only through the lens of tabloids and the rare television interview.

But the world has changed. Social media has shifted the way we view, connect with, and aspire to wealth. Today, we're living in a time where fame isn't just for movie stars and musicians; it's also for anyone who can capture attention online. Instagram, YouTube, TikTok, and Twitter have turned regular people into influencers, creating new pathways to fame and fortune that didn't exist just a few years ago. The line between celebrity and entrepreneur is blurrier than ever, with social media personalities using their platforms not just to entertain, but to build brands, launch products, and generate wealth. This chapter explores this shift, diving into how traditional celebrities have adapted to the digital era and how influencers have become the new icons of wealth.

### From Traditional Stars to Social Media Icons: The Evolution of Celebrity Wealth

Back in the day, the idea of a "celebrity" was quite narrow. If you weren't an A-list actor, a chart-topping musician, a professional athlete, or married to a president, it was nearly impossible to break into that world of fame and fortune. Let's take for example, Elizabeth Taylor—one of the most glamorous stars of her time, known not only for her acting but also for her beauty, jewels, and larger-than-life personality. People marveled at her lifestyle, her luxurious homes, and her collection of diamond jewelry, yet her world was one that fans could only glimpse from afar. There was a mystique around her that few could imagine penetrating.

Fast forward to the present, and wealth and fame have transformed into something much more interactive, immediate, and, in many ways, accessible. Now, celebrities like Kim Kardashian and Kylie Jenner use social media to share every detail of their lives—from what they eat for breakfast to the behind-the-scenes of their businesses. The mystique of old Hollywood has been replaced by a new kind of celebrity, one who is open, constantly connected, and who shares personal moments as part of their brand. The new generation of celebrities doesn't just rely on traditional media to stay relevant; they use platforms like Instagram and Twitter to stay in front of their audience every day, often monetizing their every post.

Consider Kim Kardashian, who started as a reality TV star and has since built a billion-dollar empire. Her Instagram feed is a mix of personal snapshots, promotional posts for her businesses, and glimpses of her family life. She's not just selling products; she's selling a lifestyle that millions aspire to. By sharing so much of her life, she's created a sense of intimacy with her fans that keeps them engaged—and keeps them buying.

The same goes for global icons like LeBron James and Cristiano Ronaldo, who have leveraged their sports stardom into massive online followings. LeBron is a superstar on the basketball court, but he's also a successful entrepreneur with his hands in everything from sports media to pizza franchises. Cristiano Ronaldo, with hundreds of millions of followers on Instagram, earns millions from his sponsorships and has successfully used his fame to launch his own brand of products. These athletes are no longer just sports stars; they're influencers, entrepreneurs, and wealth creators, using social media to connect with fans, promote their ventures, and build global brands.

## Celebrity Entrepreneurs: From Endorsements to Empires

In the past, celebrities primarily made money through their craft—acting, singing, or sports—and occasionally through endorsements. An athlete might appear in a Nike commercial, or an actress might promote a fragrance, but their main income came from their performances, games, or appearances. However, the celebrity business model has evolved dramatically. Today, many celebrities are not content with just endorsing products; they want to own them.

Take Sara Blakely, for example. Starting with just $5,000 in savings, Blakely founded Spanx, a shapewear company that revolutionized the fashion and apparel industry. Without any formal business training or external investors, she identified a gap in the market—comfortable, body-sculpting undergarments that catered to everyday women—and turned it into a globally recognized brand.

Blakely's success stemmed from her ingenuity and grassroots approach to marketing. Early on, she personally demonstrated her product to buyers, convincing major retailers to carry Spanx. Her ability to craft an authentic story around solving a problem resonated with consumers and helped create an entirely new product category. By maintaining full ownership of her company, Blakely not only built a billion-dollar business but also became a symbol of self-made entrepreneurial success. Her story inspires aspiring entrepreneurs by proving that innovation, perseverance, and resourcefulness can transform a simple idea into a worldwide phenomenon.

Then there's MrBeast (Jimmy Donaldson). Starting as a YouTube creator known for his outrageous challenges and philanthropic stunts, he leveraged his fame into building an empire that goes far beyond online content. With over 200 million subscribers across his channels, MrBeast didn't settle for being just a content creator—he used his massive platform to launch multiple successful business ventures, including MrBeast Burger and Feastables, a snack brand.

What sets MrBeast apart is his ability to integrate his businesses seamlessly into his content. For instance, MrBeast Burger started as a virtual restaurant brand operating through ghost kitchens, allowing fans across the U.S. to experience the brand without the need for physical locations. His snack company, Feastables, uses similar strategies, marketing directly to his loyal audience and creating viral campaigns that generate immense demand.

This new model of wealth-building—using digital fame as a launchpad for business ownership—has not only turned MrBeast into a multimillionaire but also redefined what it means to be an entrepreneur in the digital age. By leveraging his personal brand, content, and audience engagement, he exemplifies how fame can be a catalyst for long-term business success.

These celebrities exemplify a new model of wealth-building where fame is leveraged into business ownership. Rather than lending their names to other companies, they're building empires and generating lasting wealth on their own terms. The days of relying solely on endorsement deals are fading; today's celebrities are founders, CEOs, and innovators who are as much business moguls as they are entertainers.

## Influencers as Modern Icons: Wealth Through Social Media

While traditional celebrities have adapted to the digital age, a new class of wealth creators has emerged from social media. Influencers—whether on YouTube, Instagram, or TikTok—have built careers out of their online followings, proving that fame and wealth are no longer limited to Hollywood or the sports arena. Many of these influencers come from modest beginnings, yet they have used their platforms to connect with audiences, build brands, and make fortunes.

Zoe Sugg, also known as Zoella, became one of the first major influencers on YouTube. Starting with videos about beauty and lifestyle, Zoe quickly gained a massive following, which opened doors to book deals, product lines, and partnerships with major brands. She didn't come from a legacy of wealth or fame, but her genuine personality and ability to connect with viewers made her a household name in the influencer world. Today, she has a loyal fan base and a thriving business that spans beyond YouTube.

James Charles is another example of an influencer who built a career—and a substantial income—through social media. Known for his makeup tutorials and creative looks, James gained fame on Instagram and YouTube, where his bold style and skillful artistry resonated with viewers. Despite his young age, he has turned his online presence into a profitable business, securing sponsorships, brand collaborations, and even launching his own makeup line. James is not just a makeup artist; he's a brand, and his influence in the beauty industry is undeniable.

Then there's Charli D'Amelio, who skyrocketed to fame on TikTok with her dance videos. Charli's relatable personality and down-to-earth charm helped her amass millions of followers in a short period. As her popularity grew, so did her opportunities—brand deals, collaborations, and even a family reality show. She may not have a traditional background in entertainment, but Charli has become one of the most recognizable faces on social media, showing just how powerful the platform can be for wealth creation.

Influencers like Zoe, James, and Charli represent a new kind of celebrity. They may not have inherited wealth or have decades of industry experience, but their ability to connect with people online has made them incredibly influential. By sharing their lives, passions, and expertise, they've built loyal audiences that not only admire them but are also willing to support their business ventures, buy their products, and spread their messages.

## The Changing Definition of Wealth and Influence

This new era of celebrity wealth has redefined what it means to be successful. In the past, wealth was often associated with exclusivity—mansions, private islands, and a lifestyle that felt out of reach. But today's celebrities, particularly influencers, bring their followers along on their journeys, sharing both their successes and struggles. This transparency has changed how we view wealth. It's no longer just about money and possessions; it's about the ability to connect, influence, and inspire others.

This shift has significant cultural implications. As celebrities and influencers openly discuss their business strategies, investments, and financial journeys, they inspire a new generation to think differently about wealth. They've shown that wealth is not only accessible to those born into it but can also be built from scratch with creativity, passion, and the right digital tools. This has inspired countless people to pursue their dreams, take risks, and imagine new paths to success that don't necessarily follow traditional career models.

## Conclusion: The New Era of Celebrity Wealth

The world of celebrity wealth has evolved dramatically, thanks to social media and the rise of digital platforms. Traditional stars have adapted to these changes, while new influencers have emerged as modern icons of wealth and influence.

This new era of celebrity wealth has blurred the lines between fame and entrepreneurship, making wealth feel closer and more achievable than ever before. By sharing their lives and successes, these figures have transformed the way we perceive wealth, showing that it's not just about what you inherit or where you come from, but what you're willing to create and share with the world. The stage is set for a future where wealth creation is no longer exclusive to a select few, but something that feels accessible, attainable, and open to anyone with the drive and determination to make it happen.

# Chapter 6.2: The Cult of Affluence and Aspirational Lifestyle

Scroll through Instagram, TikTok, or YouTube, and it doesn't take long to find a feed filled with private jets, designer bags, glamorous vacations, and sprawling homes. Today's celebrities and influencers have perfected the art of curating lifestyles that feel effortlessly luxurious, showcasing wealth not just as something to admire, but as something to aspire to. The fantasy of wealth is no longer confined to movies or exclusive magazines; it's right there on our screens every day, making affluence feel more tangible, even attainable, if we just try hard enough.

But what's behind this fantasy of wealth, and what impact does it have on how we define success?

## Creating a Fantasy of Wealth: Selling the Dream Life

In the age of social media, creating a fantasy of wealth has become both an art and a science. Influencers and celebrities carefully curate their feeds to showcase the most glamorous aspects of their lives. This isn't just a lucky snapshot—it's often a planned photoshoot, a meticulously crafted post, or a behind-the-scenes marketing effort. These posts are designed to give us a glimpse into a lifestyle of excess, freedom, and beauty, often giving the impression that anyone could live this way with a bit of savvy branding and hard work.

Take Richard Branson, for example. His public persona is a carefully crafted blend of adventure, entrepreneurship, and luxury. Branson often shares glimpses of his extravagant lifestyle, from kite surfing on his private island, Necker Island, to piloting Virgin Galactic's spacecraft. These moments aren't random—they are part of a deliberate strategy to position himself as a modern-day adventurer and visionary.

Branson's brand message is clear: his life of luxury and excitement is the reward of bold ideas, relentless drive, and a willingness to take risks. By blending his personal exploits with his business ventures, such as Virgin Airlines, Virgin Records, and Virgin Galactic, Branson creates a narrative that wealth is not only attainable but also a gateway to extraordinary experiences. At the same time, he frequently emphasizes his humble beginnings, making his success story aspirational yet relatable to his audience. This combination of exclusivity and accessibility sells the dream that anyone, with the right mindset and courage, can achieve a life as thrilling and luxurious as his.

Similarly, travel influencers build their brand by showcasing the dreamiest parts of their adventures. Look at influencers Jack Morris and Lauren Bullen, who post breathtaking photos from locations like Bali, Greece, and the Maldives. Their lives seem to be an endless summer of beaches, sunsets, and private villas. But behind those perfect photos are sponsorships, brand deals, and extensive planning. They've created a fantasy world of travel that many people dream about, leading followers to believe that a similar lifestyle could be within reach if they too could make travel content a career.

Fitness influencers showcase luxurious home gyms, stylish athleisure, and wellness retreats, making health and fitness look like a glamorous pursuit. Interior design influencers post images of immaculate, stylish homes filled with high-end decor, giving followers ideas not just for home improvement but for what a "successful" home should look like. Across all these genres, there's a common theme: wealth and luxury are presented as accessible, attainable goals.

## A New Standard of Success: You're Only as Wealthy as You Appear

Social media has fundamentally changed what it means to be successful. In previous generations, wealth might have been discreet—a nice home, a reliable car, a comfortable life. Today, wealth is about visibility. Success isn't just about having money; it's about being seen with it. The social media era has set a new standard: wealth is something you need to show off, not just have. And if you're not visibly living that life of affluence, you're somehow less successful or less inspiring.

This aspirational model of wealth has become especially popular among young entrepreneurs and influencers. Instead of quietly working towards financial security, there's a pressure to showcase success early on. Flashy posts about "hustle culture," luxury cars, high-end fashion, and "CEO life" have flooded social media, creating a cycle where wealth isn't just personal—it's performative. Wealth is no longer something you simply achieve; it's something you market, turning success into a lifestyle brand that others want to follow.

## Instant Gratification and the Illusion of Attainability

One of the defining features of social media is its focus on instant gratification. The moment we hit "post," we can get immediate feedback in the form of likes, comments, and shares. This immediacy can make success feel closer than it actually is. When followers see influencers or celebrities flaunting their wealth online, it can feel like a quick path to riches is within reach. After all, if someone can go from a regular social media user to a millionaire influencer, why can't anyone else?

However, behind this instant visibility is often years of unseen work, brand partnerships, and an entire team of strategists and managers. The reality is far from the fantasy that social media often presents. Many of these influencers, even those who rose to fame quickly, work tirelessly to maintain their status, stay relevant, and create new content. But for followers, the illusion remains, encouraging a culture where wealth feels like it's just within reach, as long as you know how to play the social media game.

## The Psychological Impact of the Aspirational Lifestyle

This constant display of wealth and luxury has a psychological impact on viewers. When wealth is presented as not only attainable but essential to happiness and success, it creates pressure to achieve a certain lifestyle. For many, this can lead to financial strain, as they spend beyond their means trying to live up to the expectations set by influencers and celebrities.

The term "FOMO," or the fear of missing out, is particularly relevant here. When followers see their favorite influencers traveling to exotic locations, attending glamorous events, or wearing the latest designer trends, it's easy to feel like they're missing out. This can lead to a sense of dissatisfaction with one's own life, even if it's objectively fulfilling. The endless stream of aspirational content creates an unrealistic standard, where a good life isn't good enough unless it looks like a luxury lifestyle.

## Embracing Wealth Without Letting it Define Us

The aspirational lifestyle promoted by celebrities and influencers has changed the way we think about wealth, success, and happiness. While there's nothing wrong with wanting a comfortable life or even aspiring to luxury, it's important to recognize that social media often presents a filtered version of reality. The private jets, designer bags, and dream vacations are real, but they're also curated snapshots of a much more complex life.

As consumers of social media, we can appreciate these displays of wealth and beauty without letting them dictate our own sense of worth or success. True success isn't about imitating someone else's life but finding fulfillment and balance in our own. It's about defining what wealth means personally, beyond what we see on our screens. Whether it's building a meaningful career, spending time with loved ones, or achieving financial stability, real wealth is about living authentically, in a way that aligns with our values.

## Conclusion: The Cult of Affluence and Aspirational Lifestyle

The cult of affluence on social media has redefined wealth as something both glamorous and accessible, something to strive for and showcase. Celebrities and influencers have created a fantasy of wealth that, while captivating, isn't always realistic or attainable for everyone. But by being mindful of the illusions presented on social media, we can learn to appreciate the beauty of these aspirational lifestyles without feeling pressured to replicate them in our own lives.

In this new era, where wealth and success are constantly on display, it's essential to remember that real success isn't just about what we show others; it's about what truly makes us feel fulfilled. The aspirational lifestyle might be glamorous, but the real joy of life lies in authenticity, connection, and personal growth—values that go far beyond the luxury labels or exotic getaways we see online.

## Chapter 6.3: Access to Wealth: Celebrity Endorsements and Marketing

In today's world, it seems like everywhere we look, a celebrity is promoting a product, partnering with a brand, or launching a line of their own. Celebrities, with their visibility, influence, and carefully crafted images, have become more than just entertainers; they've become powerful marketers. From Beyoncé promoting her Ivy Park activewear to George Clooney co-founding Casamigos Tequila, celebrity endorsements and collaborations have become major drivers in consumer marketing. They make products desirable, add a sense of exclusivity, and, most importantly, they shape our perceptions of what it means to be successful. This chapter explores how celebrities influence our access to wealth through endorsements, collaborations, and the lifestyles they present, turning everything they touch into aspirational gold.

## The Power of Celebrity Endorsement: Selling Success by Association

Celebrity endorsements aren't new. For decades, companies have understood that associating a brand with a well-known personality can create a lasting impact. However, in the digital age, the reach and impact of these endorsements have skyrocketed. Today, celebrities are more accessible than ever. We see them on Instagram, Twitter, TikTok, and other platforms, and we feel like we "know" them, so when they endorse a product, it's like a trusted friend making a recommendation. This connection makes celebrity endorsements extremely powerful.

Think about Beyoncé and her Ivy Park line, a collaboration with Adidas. When Beyoncé promotes Ivy Park, she's not just selling clothes; she's selling a lifestyle, an attitude, and a piece of her identity. Her followers feel like they're buying into her world, and for a moment, they can imagine themselves living that glamorous life. For fans, it's not just athletic wear; it's a chance to wear something created by an icon they admire. And because Beyoncé has built a reputation for being authentic, hardworking, and powerful, those qualities get transferred to Ivy Park, making the brand irresistible to her fanbase.

Similarly, George Clooney's Casamigos Tequila isn't just another bottle on the shelf. Clooney's involvement adds a sense of sophistication and exclusivity. Clooney has a relaxed, debonair image, and Casamigos Tequila plays into that, offering the promise of sipping tequila like a

Hollywood star. Clooney and his co-founder created Casamigos originally as a private blend for friends and family, which makes consumers feel like they're being invited into an exclusive club every time they buy a bottle.

Even everyday products become aspirational when attached to a celebrity, Pepsi has a long history of working with high-profile figures. It has collaborated with everyone from Michael Jackson and Britney Spears to Cardi B. Each of these endorsements creates a powerful association in the minds of consumers. When you see your favorite celebrity enjoying Pepsi, it's easy to imagine that sipping the soda might bring a bit of their energy, fun, and success into your life.

## Why Celebrity Endorsements Work: The Power of Association

The reason celebrity endorsements are so effective lies in psychology. When a beloved celebrity promotes a product, we unconsciously associate that product with the celebrity's image. If a star is perceived as cool, sophisticated, or glamorous, those traits get transferred to the product. For example, if you see LeBron James endorsing Nike, you're likely to associate Nike with athletic excellence, strength, and achievement. Fans who look up to LeBron might feel a stronger connection to Nike because they perceive it as part of his success.

This power of association also affects how we view success and wealth. When celebrities like Beyoncé or LeBron endorse products, it's not just about the product itself—it's a signal that these items are part of the "good life." Buying these products gives fans a sense of closeness to their idols, as if they're participating in a small piece of that celebrity's world.

## Collaborations and Limited-Edition Products: Making Luxury Accessible

Celebrity collaborations have taken endorsement to a new level, transforming brands and products into high-demand luxury items. Collaborations aren't just about celebrities lending their faces to a product—they're often deeply involved in the design, concept, and branding. This makes these products feel like exclusive pieces of the celebrity's personal style and identity, making them highly desirable.

Take Kanye West's Yeezy line with Adidas. Kanye didn't just endorse Adidas; he created a brand within a brand. Yeezy sneakers have become cultural icons, known for their unique design and exclusivity. People line up and even camp out to buy the latest Yeezy drop, and the resale value of these sneakers often soars. Yeezy isn't just footwear; it's a symbol of status and coolness. Kanye's involvement gives Yeezy a sense of authenticity and uniqueness that makes fans feel like they're getting something truly special.

And then there are collaborations like Pharrell Williams with Adidas and Billionaire Boys Club. Pharrell's designs are colorful, playful, and highly personal, reflecting his unique style and artistic vision. Fans don't just buy his clothes and sneakers; they buy into his brand of creativity and individuality. Pharrell's collaborations make consumers feel like they're wearing a piece of art, something that sets them apart and gives them a sense of exclusivity.

## Limited Editions and Hype Culture

One strategy that has become increasingly popular in celebrity collaborations is the "limited edition" drop. Limited-edition products create a sense of urgency and exclusivity, as fans know that these items won't be around forever. When Kylie Jenner launches a limited-edition lip kit, for instance, fans rush to buy it before it sells out, knowing that owning it will give them a special piece of Kylie's world. Limited editions drive demand, and the hype surrounding them makes the products even more desirable.

This scarcity-based model has transformed collaborations into events. When a new Yeezy shoe or Ivy Park collection drops, it's not just a release; it's a cultural moment. Fans flood social media with their purchases, creating a buzz that further fuels demand. This "hype culture" turns buying celebrity-endorsed products into a form of social currency. It's no longer just about owning a product; it's about participating in a collective experience and showing off that participation to the world.

## Shaping Financial Aspirations: Celebrities as Wealth Role Models

Celebrities have always been aspirational figures, but today, they're shaping our financial goals in more direct ways than ever. Through their endorsements, business ventures, and social media posts, celebrities aren't just showing us their wealth—they're showing us how they made it and inviting us to follow a similar path. Many celebrities use their platforms to talk about entrepreneurship, investments, and personal branding, positioning themselves as role models for financial success.

Elon Musk isn't a traditional celebrity, but he has a massive following and wields significant influence on social media. His tweets about cryptocurrency, have had the power to shift markets. Musk frequently shares his thoughts on innovation, business, and technology, encouraging his followers to think big and take risks. He's become a symbol of ambition and financial success, inspiring countless people to pursue careers in tech and innovation.

Similarly, Jeff Bezos, Mark Zuckerberg, and other tech entrepreneurs have become symbols of modern wealth. They aren't just known for their financial success but for their entrepreneurial spirit. Many young people now see figures like Bezos and Zuckerberg as role models, not just for building wealth, but for building something meaningful from scratch. Their journeys from modest beginnings to billion-dollar empires have inspired a generation to think differently about wealth and success, pushing them to consider entrepreneurship, innovation, and investment.

For a slightly different example, consider Oprah Winfrey. She has used her platform to inspire financial literacy and personal growth. Through her books, TV shows, and public speaking, Oprah has consistently shared messages about empowerment, resilience, and the importance of financial independence. She's a billionaire, but she's also relatable to her fans, showing that it's possible to build wealth while staying true to one's values. Oprah's influence has led many of her followers to take control of their finances, focus on self-improvement, and aim for success in ways that are meaningful to them.

## Celebrity Brands as Financial Aspirations

When celebrities create successful brands, they often share parts of their journey, giving fans a sense of how they achieved their wealth.

One great example of this is Dwayne "The Rock" Johnson and his tequila brand, Teremana. The Rock shares his passion for the brand, along with stories about the tequila-making process and his hands-on approach to building the business. He's made his brand personal, inviting fans to join him in his journey and enjoy his product. By doing so, The Rock has transformed Teremana into more than just tequila; it's a symbol of his work ethic, ambition, and pursuit of excellence. Fans who admire him feel like they're part of his journey when they buy Teremana, which reinforces their aspirations to emulate his success.

## Conclusion: The Influence of Celebrity Endorsements on Our Aspirations and Lifestyles

Celebrity endorsements, collaborations, and personal brands have a profound impact on how we view wealth and success. When we see our favorite celebrities promoting products or launching businesses, it's easy to buy into the fantasy that we, too, can live a life of affluence and luxury. Celebrity endorsements make products aspirational, collaborations add a sense of exclusivity, and celebrities themselves have become role models for financial ambition, shaping our views on what it means to be wealthy.

The power of celebrity influence extends beyond the products they promote. By watching celebrities build brands, engage in entrepreneurship, and share their journeys, we're encouraged to think bigger, take risks, and pursue financial independence. However, it's also essential to remember that these portrayals are often polished, curated, and designed to drive consumer behavior. While celebrities can be sources of inspiration, their success is unique to their circumstances and doesn't always reflect the challenges of building wealth in real life.

As consumers, we can appreciate and be inspired by the success stories of celebrities without feeling pressured to achieve the same levels of wealth or status. True success lies not in emulating someone else's life but in finding our own path, values, and fulfillment.

# The Legacy of the New Gilded Age

In many ways, we're living in a moment that feels reminiscent of the original Gilded Age—a period in the late 19th century marked by rapid industrialization, massive wealth accumulation, and an obsession with opulence. Back then, it was the Carnegies, the Vanderbilts, and the Rockefellers who became the icons of wealth and influence. Today, it's the tech moguls, social media stars, and entrepreneurial celebrities who have stepped into the spotlight, reshaping our perception of what it means to be successful. Yet, while the names and industries have changed, the fascination with wealth, luxury, and status remains.

We're witnessing an era where wealth feels closer and more accessible, and in some ways, it is. Thanks to social media, we get daily glimpses into the lives of the ultra-wealthy. We see their vacations, their homes, their cars, and their wardrobes, making it easy to aspire to similar levels of success. Tech billionaires share their startup stories, influencers launch businesses from their bedrooms, and the financial elite showcase their lifestyles in ways that feel both inspiring and daunting. The American Dream, which once focused on modest success and financial stability, has expanded into something grander, more glamorous, and, for many, seemingly within reach.

But this new Gilded Age isn't just about personal ambition or chasing wealth. As it unfolds, it's leaving a mark on American culture and values that will shape how future generations understand success, fulfillment, and the very idea of the American Dream. If we look closely, we can see that today's Gilded Age is influencing much more than personal finance or social media feeds—it's redefining how we think about status, achievement, and even happiness.

In this chapter, we'll explore the cultural legacy of our modern Gilded Age. Just as the original era left a complex legacy of both progress and inequality, our current moment is poised to impact society on many levels. We'll dive into how this cultural shift is reshaping the aspirations of young people, influencing family values, and redefining what it means to "make it" in America. We'll also consider the broader societal and environmental implications, as today's fast-paced wealth creation raises questions about sustainability, ethical responsibility, and social equity.

One of the core questions of this chapter is: What does it mean for the American Dream when the pathway to wealth seems increasingly tied to personal branding, viral fame, or having the next big idea? In the past, the dream was often defined by home ownership, stable income, and the promise of a better life for one's children. But as the definitions of success have shifted, so too have the symbols associated with that dream. For some, the markers of success have become less about security and more about visibility—being seen as successful rather than simply being comfortable. When everyone has a window into the lives of the rich and famous, wealth becomes less of a private achievement and more of a social statement, changing not only what people aspire to but also how they define themselves.

However, as with any era of rapid wealth accumulation, this one brings its own set of challenges and potential pitfalls. While we celebrate the rise of self-made millionaires and applaud the entrepreneurial spirit of our time, we also face stark contrasts in wealth distribution. Not everyone has the resources to access these new pathways to success, and the wealth gap continues to widen. What happens when the glamorized, accessible wealth of a few starts to cast a shadow over those who struggle to make ends meet? And how will this age of affluence impact the American identity in the long term?

Beyond economic inequality, there are also pressing questions about sustainability and the ethical responsibilities of wealth. As we see a cultural shift toward excess and luxury, there is growing concern about the environmental and social impacts of such lifestyles. Will future generations inherit a legacy of consumption and waste, or will this era ultimately inspire a reevaluation of what wealth and success should mean in a rapidly changing world?

As we journey through this chapter, we'll reflect on how future generations might interpret this new Gilded Age. Will they view it as a time of bold ambition and self-empowerment? Or will they see it as a period of imbalance, where the pursuit of affluence overshadowed values like community, equity, and sustainability? Much like the original Gilded Age, this moment in history will be remembered for its innovations, its glamour, and its extraordinary wealth—but it will also be scrutinized for its societal impacts, its inequities, and its enduring influence on the American psyche.

The legacy of the new Gilded Age isn't written yet, but the decisions we make, the values we uphold, and the aspirations we set will shape how this era is remembered. Future generations will inherit not just the symbols of our success, but also the consequences of our choices, and it's up to us to consider the impact of both. As we explore the cultural ramifications of this modern-day gilded era, we'll consider how to build a future that values not only wealth but also wisdom, compassion, and collective responsibility.

## Chapter 7.1: The Cultural Shift Toward Wealth and Luxury

In recent years, wealth and luxury have become not just symbols of success, but cultural pursuits in their own right. Luxury isn't only for the elite anymore; it's everywhere we look. We see it on social media, in movies, in travel blogs, and even on our own feeds, where friends and family are posting snapshots from their latest vacations, luxury purchases, and gourmet meals. Luxury has moved from something reserved for the few to an aspirational goal for the many. It's no longer just a byproduct of wealth; it's something to be actively pursued and displayed.

The shift isn't just about access; it's about what wealth and luxury represent today. Luxury has become less about exclusive, private moments of indulgence and more about public displays and shared experiences. Whether it's jetting off to Bali for a yoga retreat, staying at a chic boutique hotel, or getting the latest iPhone, luxury today has a new face—one that's increasingly accessible, visible, and, perhaps most importantly, shareable. Let's examine how this cultural shift toward wealth and luxury has evolved, why it matters, and what it means for the generations growing up in this era of hyper-visible affluence.

## Luxury as a Cultural Pursuit: The Democratization of Opulence

In the past, luxury was a world that seemed light-years away for most people. We might have glimpsed it in movies or glossy magazines, but the mansions, yachts, and private jets belonged to a rarefied circle—the ultra-wealthy whose lives were as unreachable as they were glamorous. Today, however, luxury has taken on a more approachable quality. The lines between exclusive and accessible have blurred, largely thanks to social media and digital marketing. We don't just see luxury; we're encouraged to believe it's within reach if we work hard enough or save strategically.

Gucci, Louis Vuitton, and Chanel used to be brands that only the wealthiest could afford. Today, these brands are frequently featured in the posts of influencers across Instagram, TikTok, and YouTube, often with sponsored content or "unboxing" videos that showcase the latest fashion or handbag as something anyone can aspire to own. By partnering with influencers who represent a broader demographic than Hollywood celebrities or Wall Street moguls, these brands have made luxury feel relatable and achievable. When you see your favorite lifestyle influencer sporting a Louis Vuitton bag, it's easier to imagine that with some saving or credit, you too could buy into that experience.

Another area where luxury has become democratized is travel. High-end resorts and unique travel experiences that used to feel out of reach are now featured prominently on social media, with influencers sharing curated moments from exotic destinations and boutique hotels. Influencers often stay at these locations as part of collaborations, making luxury travel feel accessible, even if the costs are still high. For those who can't afford the full experience, there are still options to book similar stays on a smaller scale or to partake in mini-versions of these luxury experiences. Airbnb, for example, offers "Airbnb Luxe" properties, which allow more people to experience upscale accommodations, often at a fraction of the cost of traditional luxury hotels.

And it's not just about products and travel. Experiences themselves have become commodified and branded as luxury. From personalized workout sessions to gourmet meal delivery services, luxury today includes a wide range of experiences that can make anyone feel part of a more exclusive world. Even fitness and wellness have joined the luxury trend—consider boutique fitness studios SoulCycle, Barry's Bootcamp, or private yoga instructors who provide not just exercise but a high-end experience that comes with a social status. Luxury is no longer just about owning expensive things; it's about curating a lifestyle that feels sophisticated and elevated.

## Symbolism of Wealth in the Modern Era: Experiences Over Possessions

In this modern age, wealth isn't only about physical assets such as homes, cars, or jewelry. Increasingly, it's about access, exclusivity, and, most importantly, experiences. Today's wealthy are just as likely to invest in luxury experiences as they are in tangible assets. And these experiences are as much a part of their identity as any physical possession.

Social media has played a significant role in this shift by making it easy for people to share their experiences with a broad audience. For instance, attending exclusive events, dining at high-end restaurants, or staying in luxurious resorts has become part of the vocabulary of wealth. Sharing these experiences has become a way for people to signal their status without the need for traditional wealth markers like private jets or palatial mansions.

A great example of this is the rise of "luxury experiences" in travel. People are increasingly valuing unique, high-end travel experiences over traditional material symbols of wealth. Instead of owning a vacation home, many affluent people today prefer to spend money on curated travel experiences that they can share on social media. Going on a wellness retreat in Bali, attending a private chef's dinner in Paris, or scuba diving in a remote part of the Maldives isn't just about relaxation—it's about signaling a lifestyle that values exclusivity, adventure, and uniqueness.

Technology has also joined the ranks of modern luxury symbols. Take the Apple ecosystem, for example. Owning the latest iPhone, MacBook, or Apple Watch is more than just a tech choice; it's a status symbol that communicates a certain level of affluence. By releasing new models each year, Apple taps into the desire for the latest and greatest, creating a culture where having the newest device represents social standing. Similarly, other high-end technology brands, like Tesla, have made luxury cars accessible to a broader audience, allowing more people to enjoy and display a luxury lifestyle in a modern, eco-conscious way.

This shift toward experiential luxury also points to a broader cultural change: we now equate wealth with the ability to curate an extraordinary lifestyle. Wealth today is less about buying things and more about doing things—things that are beautiful, unique, and often highly Instagrammable. This shift in symbols isn't only reshaping how we view wealth; it's setting new cultural standards for success that prioritize access to experiences over traditional assets.

## Materialism and the Pursuit of Status: The Pressure to Keep Up

While luxury may be more accessible, this trend comes with its own set of pressures. As wealth becomes more visible on social media, there's a natural desire to keep up with these often-idealized portrayals of success. The line between inspiration and comparison blurs, leading many to feel that they, too, need to present an affluent lifestyle to keep up with social expectations or to feel validated in their achievements.

This visibility can contribute to a culture of materialism, where the pursuit of status symbols and luxurious experiences becomes a driving force in people's lives. Instagram, which encourage users to share and celebrate their successes and high points, often end up fostering a sense of competition. It's no longer just about enjoying a nice vacation or buying a new car—it's about making sure that others see these achievements. The result is a culture that prioritizes external validation over personal fulfillment, leading many to spend more on "keeping up" than on things that truly bring them joy.

Take, for instance, the trend of "unboxing" videos on YouTube, where influencers open and showcase high-end products. While these videos can be fun and informative, they can also spark a sense of desire and inadequacy among viewers who feel like they need those items to be happy or successful. And it's not limited to luxury items. Influencers unbox everything from designer bags to high-tech gadgets to trendy home decor, giving viewers the impression that these things are essential parts of a modern, successful lifestyle.

The desire to keep up with these ideals isn't just a financial issue—it's a psychological one. Constant exposure to curated, idealized lifestyles can lead to feelings of inadequacy and even anxiety. When wealth and luxury are visible and celebrated all around us, it's easy to feel like we're falling behind if we're not living up to those same standards. Social media becomes a highlight reel of other people's best moments, leaving some people feeling as if they'll never be able to match up to the "ideal" lives they see online.

## Finding Balance in the Pursuit of Wealth and Luxury

As luxury becomes more visible and accessible, it's crucial to remember that true fulfillment doesn't come from simply mimicking the lifestyles we see on social media. While there's nothing wrong with enjoying luxury or aspiring to success, it's essential to keep these pursuits in perspective. Wealth and luxury should be sources of enjoyment, not pressure or validation.

For many, the answer lies in finding a balance—learning to appreciate the inspiration that luxury culture offers without feeling the need to constantly keep up. Luxury can be a beautiful part of life, but it's only one piece of the puzzle. Real fulfillment comes from a blend of experiences, relationships, achievements, and personal values that go beyond what's on our social media feeds.

In the end, this cultural shift toward wealth and luxury presents both opportunities and challenges. It allows more people to enjoy and aspire to beautiful experiences, but it also places pressure on us to keep up with standards that might not be realistic or sustainable. As we move forward, finding a balanced approach to wealth, success, and luxury will be key to creating a culture that values both affluence and authenticity.

# CONCLUSION:

# The Long Reach of the Gilded Revival

The era we're living in now feels like a revival of the Gilded Age—a time when rapid wealth accumulation, technological leaps, and an obsession with luxury reshaped America. This modern Gilded Age isn't just about the ultra-rich or famous; it's about how we as a society have come to define success, ambition, and the "good life." It's about the way we've embraced wealth as a symbol, not just of financial security, but as an aspirational lifestyle—a set of experiences, luxuries, and accomplishments to be shared and admired. As we reach the end of this exploration, it's time to reflect on what this Gilded Revival means for the future.

Will it be remembered as a transformative era that reshaped the American Dream for the better? Or will it be viewed as a time of extreme wealth inequality, where the pursuit of opulence left lasting scars on society? The legacy of this age will depend largely on the choices we make now as individuals and as a society. Let's take a closer look at how the symbols, values, and social dynamics of this new Gilded Age will likely shape the future.

## Redefining Success and the New American Dream

For decades, the American Dream was about finding stability—owning a modest home, having a steady job, and securing a better life for future generations. In our current Gilded Revival, that dream has evolved. Success today isn't just about stability; it's about standing out, creating a lifestyle that feels unique and enviable. Social media has shifted our goals from private accomplishments to public displays, where the things we own, the places we go, and the life we showcase are all part of a carefully curated image.

Consider the way success is portrayed on Instagram and TikTok. People share luxury vacations, entrepreneurial ventures, and daily snapshots that show not only what they're doing but what they're aspiring to. It's not enough to be successful—you have to be seen as successful. This shift has turned traditional markers of wealth, like a nice house or a reliable car, into grander symbols: high-rise condos, designer clothes, and private islands are the new benchmarks. Even for those who aren't famous or wealthy, there's a pressure to project an image of affluence.

This evolution of the American Dream has both positive and negative effects. On the one hand, it's empowering to know that wealth is more accessible, at least symbolically, and that success can be built from anywhere with enough creativity, hustle, and social savvy. The stories of influencers and entrepreneurs going from obscurity to affluence inspire many people to dream bigger. On the other hand, the constant comparison that social media enables can lead to burnout, dissatisfaction, and a never-ending chase for "more." The question moving forward will be: Can we balance the pursuit of success with a sense of personal fulfillment, or will the pressure to keep up take a significant toll on our well-being?

## The Rise of the Wealth Gap and Social Inequality

One of the most significant issues with any Gilded Age, past or present, is the wealth gap. Today, despite the sense that anyone can become wealthy with enough effort or the right idea, the reality is that wealth inequality continues to grow. A small percentage of individuals control a disproportionate amount of wealth, while many Americans struggle with financial instability.

If this new Gilded Age is to leave a positive legacy, it will require meaningful efforts to bridge this divide. That could mean changes in how we approach taxation, how companies invest in their communities, or how we, as a society, recognize and reward contributions to the common good. Perhaps the tech entrepreneurs, celebrities, and financial moguls of today will set new standards by using their wealth and influence to drive social progress. Already, figures like Bill Gates, who has dedicated much of his fortune to philanthropy, show that it's possible for the ultra-wealthy to make a positive impact. But the choice between legacy and excess is a personal one, and it remains to be seen how many of today's wealthy will prioritize long-term societal impact over personal gain.

## Social Responsibility and the Future of Wealth

One of the defining questions for this era will be: How will those with wealth choose to use it? There's been a cultural shift toward recognizing the responsibility that comes with affluence, especially as global issues like climate change, social justice, and poverty demand urgent attention. Some of the wealthiest individuals and companies have committed to sustainable practices, ethical investing, and philanthropy. However, while there are leaders in social responsibility, the vast influence of corporate and personal wealth also raises concerns about accountability.

Think of companies like Patagonia, which have embedded environmental responsibility into their brand identity. They've shown that it's possible to be both successful and principled, and their choices have inspired consumers and other companies alike to consider sustainability. Similarly, celebrities like Leonardo DiCaprio, who advocates for environmental protection, and Rihanna, who has used her platform to promote social causes, show how wealth and influence can be channeled for positive change.

## The Role of Technology in Shaping the Future

Technology is one of the defining features of this modern Gilded Age. It's not only transformed industries but also changed the way we live, work, and socialize. Innovations in social media, artificial intelligence, and digital finance have made it easier to create and manage wealth. But with these advancements come new challenges—ethical dilemmas about privacy, questions about the role of AI in employment, and concerns about how technology contributes to the wealth gap.

Consider the role of social media influencers, who, through YouTube and Instagram, have created new pathways to wealth. These platforms have democratized fame, giving people from all walks of life the chance to reach millions. But there's a darker side too: the mental health impacts of being constantly "on," the algorithm-driven pressure to outdo each post, and the sometimes toxic culture of comparison. Technology has made wealth creation more accessible, but it has also introduced new stresses and expectations, particularly for younger generations.

Future generations will inherit these tools and likely build upon them in ways we can't yet imagine. But they'll also have to grapple with the ethical and social consequences that come with a tech-driven economy. The legacy of this Gilded Age will be shaped not just by wealth but by how we choose to use technology to support or hinder a fair, balanced society.

## Redefining Wealth for the 21st Century

One of the most important aspects of the legacy of this Gilded Revival will be how we redefine wealth itself. Historically, wealth was about accumulation, ownership, and sometimes even secrecy. Today, it's increasingly about visibility, influence, and lifestyle. The wealthy don't just live in gated mansions anymore; they live online, sharing their lives, their causes, and their ideas with millions.

This shift toward transparency could be a force for good if it encourages a more open, responsible form of wealth. Younger generations seem more interested in experiences, social impact, and personal freedom than in accumulating possessions. This trend could redefine what it means to be wealthy in the 21st century—moving from materialism toward meaning, from status symbols toward purpose-driven success.

Ultimately, the legacy of this modern Gilded Age will be about more than dollars and cents. It will be about how we choose to value ourselves, each other, and the world we share. Will wealth continue to be a tool for personal gain, or can it become a force for collective well-being? Can we embrace the luxuries of life without losing sight of the values that make it meaningful?

## Final Reflections: Choosing Our Legacy

As we close this exploration of the Gilded Revival, one thing is clear: the choices we make today will define the world we leave behind. This era could be remembered as a time of bold ambition, creativity, and progress, or as a period of excess, inequality, and missed opportunities.

We stand at a crossroads where the future of wealth, success, and the American Dream is being reimagined. What it becomes next depends on our ability to question, adapt, and make choices that go beyond just what we want—to include what we're responsible for. In a world that often measures us by what we have, it's worth asking: who are we, and who do we want to be?